MW00460807

You Can Fly Beyond the Sky!

*Quick, Simple and Powerful Strategies
Toward the Fulfillment of Your Dreams,
Goals, and Aspirations*

Isaac "Dr. O" Olatunji Jr., Ph.D,

Dr. O Publishing
Huntsville, AL

Unless otherwise indicated, all scriptural quotations are from the *King James Version* of the Bible.

You Can Fly Beyond the Sky!
Published by:
Dr. O Publishing
P.O. Box 30033
7000 Adventist Blvd. NW
Huntsville, AL 35896

ISBN 0-9742841-0-6

Third Printing, April, 2007

Book production by:
Silver Lining Creative
www.silverliningcreative.com

Printed in the United States of America.

Dedication

Dedicated to My Fellow Dreamers!
In memory of Carmen Brooks Olatunji

— 1947-1995

Contents

Acknowledgements

A special thank you to the following individuals who have made this project possible:

Dexter and Sylvia Wright, CEO/COO
Terrell A Enterprises
Your contribution towards this project will never be forgotten.

Drs. Norman and Lorraine Stiggers

Your optimism, prayers and encouragement in my time of need will always be appreciated. Thank you for those words of faith that propelled me to write this project.

To all my family, friends and colleagues. May God Truly and Richly Bless You!

Last and Most Important...God the Father, Jesus Christ — His Son and The Holy Spirit, My Father, Saviour, Teacher and Motivator. Thank you for making the provision for this vision!

Testimonials

"You Can Fly Beyond the Sky" is written in a motivational format, geared towards Christians, those seeking advice or reassurance in life, those seeking answers to their purpose and those willing to make changes in their life. The author utilizes stories to pull the reader into the text and show them successful and simple ways to change their lives. Through reading the text, the reader will feel as though they can hear the author cheering and pushing them along their path to greatness.

> —Natasha Munson, publicist and best selling author of the book, "Life Lessons for My Black Girls", published by Writers Club Press.

Dr. O's book was a true eye opener and confirmed what was in my heart all along that I am destined to be great!... This book serves as a road map to help you on the path to bringing your dreams into fruition. "You Can Fly Beyond the Sky" is chock full of specifics on how you can develop your dreams and along the way continually build and strengthen your relationship with God, our Creator. I encourage you to read this book with an open mind and like the old adage goes, "the only one that can stop you is you."

> —V. Frazier, Chicago, IL

This book is one of the best books that I've read this year! I will be putting the One Week Empowerment Challenge into practice this week.

—N. Birdsong, Los Angeles, CA

This book was AWESOME!!!! It has really blessed me and I am looking forward to reading it again and again. The information contained in this book is exactly what I need to encourage me that I can fly beyond the sky and achieve the goals and dreams that I have regardless of any setbacks, or current situations that may seem to stand in the way of achieving my goals. One thing that I found so impressive about the book was the order in which it was written. The fact that the book was written for any reader regardless of their religion or lifestyle is an A+!

—K. Rideaux, Louisiana

I really enjoyed your book...I found myself unable to put it down. Your inspiring motivation has ignited a fire in me that had almost dwindled completely out. It was just what I needed when I needed it the most. I thank you for your gifts, talents, ambition, drive, motivation, passion and FIRE for a more positive lifestyle. You are a true, true inspiration.

—Tulsa, OK

"In the common walks of life there is many a man patiently treading the round of daily toil, unconscious that he possesses powers which, if called into action, would raise him to an equality with the world's most honored men. The touch of a skillful hand is needed to arouse those dormant faculties."

— *E. G. White*

Introduction

A Call To Take Action

Friend, what is the aim and purpose of your life? Do you desire to soar above the circumstances that now surround you? Are you ambitious for education so that you may have a name and position? Do you have thoughts that you dare not express, thoughts that you may one day stand upon the summit of greatness and achieve your life's dreams? There is nothing wrong with having these aspirations. Every one of you may make your mark! Do not settle for low attainments. Aim high, fly beyond the sky, and spare no pains to reach the standard!

This book is a call for you to take action and to fly beyond the sky! You are the masterpiece of Creation! You were made in the image of God. You have powers and abilities only waiting the touch of the skillful hand of the Creator to elevate you to higher heights in the fulfillment of your dreams! You were not created for failure! With God there is no failure! To put your dream into His hands is a 1000 percent guarantee of success in pursuing your dreams. Many feel that their dreams are far beyond their ability to achieve. But friend, this book has been written to inspire you that with God's help you can fly beyond the sky toward the fulfillment of your dreams!

The book that you now have in your hands contains seven empowerment strategies leading you to the *power source* that will give you the power to achieve your dreams. The principles contained in this book are based upon practical, universal strategies given by the greatest Teacher who ever lived. These strategies constitute the foundation of true success not only in this life but in the life to come. The purpose of this book is to inspire readers to achieve their dreams by using its everlasting principles. You cannot lose if you utilize these principles! You are guaranteed success in any line of work, dream, or purpose that you aspire to.

This book is a straightforward, no-nonsense approach outlining the eternal principles that the Creator has ordained for those who are serious about changing their lives and leaving the cage of unfulfilled dreams to soar beyond the sky! Napoleon Hill once said, "You can if you believe you can." Jesus said, "All things are possible to him that believeth."

This book is a book on applied faith, taking the principles of the Bible, psychology, and practical common sense that will lead readers to understand that with God's help, coupled with faith and earnest effort, they can rise above their present circumstances and achieve whatever their hearts desire. I am confident that you will be inspired and empowered as you read and utilize the principles contained in this book. My prayer is not only will you be successful in this life, but that you will have an intimate walk with the One who gets all the credit, God your Creator — the power source of your dreams and aspirations. Friend, prepare and get ready to leave your cage and fly beyond the sky as you read this book.

— *Isaac "Dr. O" Olatunji Jr., Ph.D.*
Life Empowerment Strategist

Strategy #1
Believe That You Can Fly

Do you know that you can fly beyond the sky? If you have doubts, learn from this analogy concerning the eagle. The eagle, by instinct, flies as high as he desires. He doesn't think about his limitations when it comes to flying. He only does what his Creator has empowered him to do. The eagle is empowered to fly, and nothing hinders him from making his upward flight.

You Are an Eagle!

You are an eagle. You can fly beyond the sky! You were created by God to soar beyond the sky when it comes to achieving your life's dreams and goals. The problem with many today is the fact that they are living in a chicken pen, not knowing the power they have as an eagle.

The story is told of an eagle's egg that wound up in a chicken pen. The mother hen, not knowing the difference between the eagle's egg and her eggs, sat on it. Eventually it hatched, and an eagle sprang forth. The baby eagle was raised as a chicken, and for a long time he believed that he *was* a chicken, not knowing that he could fly. For years, this eagle, living in a chicken pen, thought as a chicken, and acted like a chicken, not knowing the potential he had for soaring higher.

One day an eagle was flying over the pen, noticed one of his kind below, and politely flew down and greeted his fellow eagle. The eagle that had lived for years in the chicken pen responded to him as a chicken and this startled the other eagle.

The older eagle realized that the young eagle had been conditioned through his environment and upbringing to think of himself as a chicken. He did not blame the young eagle for thinking like a chicken. Instead, this older eagle taught the younger one to believe in the abilities of his nature and potential as an eagle and to believe that he could fly above the chicken pen where he had been kept in bondage. To the chicken-eagle, this revelation, though painful, was the beginning of his rising above the thinking and environment that had formally shaped his thinking. He began thinking like an eagle, and eventually he began to fly like an eagle and to soar to higher heights.

Does this sound like you? Are you in a chicken pen of circumstances due to birth, heredity, environment, or your perceived "misfortunes" in life? Whatever it may be or appears to be, you must understand the fact that you are an eagle! You were created and empowered by God to soar beyond the sky. You do not have to remain where you are in life. Fate has not tied knots so firmly around your circumstances to the extent that you must remain in bondage.

I now want to relate the story of a man who soared beyond the sky by utilizing his God-given potential to achieve his dreams.

A Man Who Thought and Grew Rich

The life of S. B. Fuller, a successful soap salesman, is an inspirational story about a man who, although he was born and raised in poverty, did not allow his circumstances to keep him from becoming a millionaire through a little inspiration and a lot of faith.

Fuller, an African-American, was born the son of a tenant farmer in Louisiana, and began to work at the age of five. At that time, many tenant farmer families accepted poverty as their lot and did not aspire to do better. The difference in this story was that Fuller's mother gave him an inspiring thought that stayed with him throughout his life. This thought changed his whole life and eventually raised him from rags to riches.

"We shouldn't be poor, S. B.," Mrs Fuller said to her son. "And don't ever let me hear you say that it is God's will that we are poor. We are poor, but not because of God. We are poor because your father has never developed a desire to become rich. No one in our family has ever developed a desire to be anything else."

This thought was the beginning of the desire in S. B. Fuller's life to strive for something better. He wanted to be rich, and his desire to succeed became such a burning passion in him that he went forward and achieved his life's dream.

When he become older and was on his own, he figured out a service that he could perform to earn money. He fell in love with the trade of selling soap. Realizing that people become dirty and need good soap, Fuller became a door-to-door soap salesman. For 12 years he diligently sold soap for the soap company that he worked for.

When the soap company came up for sale, Fuller desired to buy it. He had about $25,000 in savings from his years of sales, and he used this as his down payment, promising to obtain the remaining $125,000 that he needed to buy the company and become its

3

sole owner. Because of his good name, he obtained money from friends and loans from companies and investment groups. He received all the money except for $10,000 to achieve the dream of a lifetime.

But Fuller did not give up. He prayed and God answered his prayer in the form of a check for $10,000 from a contractor! Fuller bought the company and became a business tycoon, selling soap products. He left the chicken pen of poverty and soared to higher heights because he desired, believed, and finally achieved his heart's desire to do something better in life with faith and effort!

How is it with you my friend? You may be in binding circumstances in life as you read these words, but I tell you that you do not have to remain in the chicken pen of your situation. You can fly beyond the sky! Master your circumstances; do not allow your circumstances to master you! Take charge of your life. Tell God and yourself that a change is coming! Then act upon your dreams and goals and watch miracles happen.

Take Control of Your Life

What is your heart's desire in life? What goals do you want to achieve? How much money would you like to earn this year? Where do you want to be five years from now? Whatever desires, dreams and goals you may have, you must remember that you can achieve all that your heart desires as long as it does not violate the laws of God or the rights of your fellow man. And just like the eagle, you can soar to higher heights in your life's achievements.

This book is that fellow eagle that will teach you about your God-given potential and will lead you to soar to higher heights. You were created in the image of God, to reflect His character and to glorify Him. He endowed you with the true power within--the power of choice to formulate character.

What is character? Character is what you think, what you speak, what you do. Finally, character is who you are. What are your thoughts like? What are your feelings like? What words of prophecy have you spoken into your life? What are you?

You are the total sum of your thoughts expressed in words and actions that have made you what you are. That is your character, and it all begins and ends in your mind. The Bible is correct in stating, "As a man thinketh in his heart, so is he." You are what you think. The body with all its functions was created to serve as the carrier and achiever of all the mind's thoughts.

Whatever you thought yourself to be is exactly what you are. You cannot blame the circumstances of your birth, environment, heredity, family, friends, job, race, etc., for who you are. No, you are what you are because you made yourself what you are. External conditions, heredity, and life experiences may have played a part in forming your character, but the crux of the matter is, the one who formed your character is you!

When we discuss flying beyond the sky to achieve our goals and dreams, we must take personal responsibility for achieving them. We cannot blame any external conditions for not achieving them. We must take the responsibility for all our actions. When we take responsibility for our lives and do not blame someone or something else for how our lives are and are how they are to be, we can begin the journey to successful life achievement.

A Man Who Took Control of His Life

In the state of Kentucky there once lived a 65-year-old man who was flat broke when he retired.

When he received his first Social Security check, it amounted to a little over $100. Frustrated with this check and rightfully so, he decided to take control of his life. He sought to make a fortune from a recipe for fried chicken that he believed would sell in restaurants. So he went across the nation, a broke 65-year - old man, in a beat-up old car.

For two years he went from restaurant owner to restaurant owner, seeking an entrance into the food industry with his "million-dollar recipe." After more than 1,000 rejections, he finally received a yes answer, and that yes opened the door for Colonel Sanders to amass a multi-million-dollar fortune. Kentucky Fried Chicken to this day still rates among the top fast food businesses in the world.

This is so because a man had a dream that a simple recipe he believed in would sell and lift him from the "earth" of a dismal Social Security check to the "stratosphere" of millions of dollars. This is so because Colonel Sanders decided to take control of the circumstances of his life. He could have allowed life to ride him in his poverty, but he chose to ride life, and he persevered until his dream came true!

Many people could not have endured the 1,000 rejections that Colonel Sanders received, but he applied the principle of perseverance until someone said yes. Many would have given up in discouragement long before rejection 100, but the point is that *applied faith backed with perseverance will eventually lead to the bright light at the end of the tunnel.*

The Power of Your Mind

Your *words* are *verbal* expressions of your mind. Your *actions* are *physical* expressions of your mind. The Bible says, "Out of the heart are the issues of life." The heart or the mind is where your life's dreams and goals begin. It is through the right use of the mind, aided by divine wisdom, that your dreams begin their path to fulfillment.

The mind, the center of all life--from whence all life issues, problems and dreams spring — was given by our Creator for us to use correctly and to achieve all that it can conceive, as long as it will not violate His will and the rights of our fellow man. It is a true saying that "Whatever the mind can conceive, it surely can achieve."

We see so much evil in our world, including crime, war, and violence, but has anyone stopped to ponder where all of this comes from? The answer is simple: It lies within the mind.

God has endowed man with the ability to bring all he sees into fruition. God has given us the power of choice, to think and to do. He could have made all of us to be robots and do whatever He commanded without our thinking about it. But the problem with that would have been that man would not have developed the powerful mind that God had given him to use. His mind would have been powerless, thereby making man powerless.

The United Negro College Fund was right on target when it said, "A mind is a terrible thing to waste." If you fail to exercise the mind power the Creator has given you, your mind will become powerless, making you and your dreams the same — powerless!

If you bind a broken arm in a cast, after awhile the arm becomes powerless, and you will need a sling to carry it. It reminds me of when I was seven years old, playing with some friends on a tree. I jumped off a limb to swing onto another, and I missed the limb and fell to the ground. I dislocated my right elbow. As a result of this unfortunate accident, I had to wear a cast for two weeks. At the end of those two weeks, my cast was taken off and my right arm was completely power-less due to lack of use. I had to wear a sling for anoth-er week or so before my arm became strong enough to use again.

This analogy is the same with our minds when it comes to achieving our life's dreams. If we do not use our minds to achieve them, the mind becomes power-less, and then we lean on others' thoughts about our dreams and goals. Thus, we become slaves to other men's thoughts, and the dream in your heart becomes extinguished. My friend, this must not be, and this will not be if you really desire it.

I believe you are ready for a change, because you are now reading this book. Reading the principles contained in it will empower you to achieve your life's goals, but it will never substitute for what *you* must do — which is to *work!*

"Faith without works is dead" is the sign that hangs in the exercise studio of Billy Blanks, creator of Tae-Bo, the famous exercise workout. Billy's philoso-phy of exercise and achieving health goals is centered in that one statement. If you desire to lose weight or to be physically fit, you must put your works where your faith is. To say it another way, you must do your part to bring the results you desire.

Dr. Dennis Kimbro, in his best-selling book, *Think and Grow Rich — A Black Choice,* states it in a more powerful way: "Pray as it all depended upon God, and work as if it all depended upon you." These are words of wisdom we can learn from when it comes to achieving our life's goals.

In the first pages of Napoleon Hill's book, *Think and Grow Rich*, he states the key to attaining riches. I believe his philosophy of attaining riches is the same for achieving your life's dreams. Dr. Hill said, "All achievement, all earned riches, have their beginning in an idea! If you are ready for the secret, you already possess one half of it; therefore, you will readily recognize the other half the moment it reaches your mind." The other half of life achievement brought out by Dr. Hill is summarized throughout his book as persistent, applied faith! You can have faith, but if it is not backed up by persistent action, then that faith is dead; therefore, your dreams become nothing more than wishful thinking.

Get to the Goal Line

One common element which separates achievers from non-achievers is the fact that achievers had an idea, stuck to it and succeeded, while the others either had an idea and did not follow through on it or they did follow through on it, but they did not persist long enough to achieve their heart's desire.

NBA star Allen Iverson brought out this truth by saying, "The only person that can stop me, is me!" Friend, the only person who can stop you from achieving your life's dreams is you! There is no one who can stop you. You are at the 50-yard line. You began at the one-yard line. You have an idea, a dream, and a goal that you desire to achieve. That idea has put you halfway between you and the goal line. There is nothing but an open field before you, and all that can stop you are the defensive players of fear, doubt, lack of vision, and procrastination. They are just an arm's length from grabbing and stopping you, but you have the power of will to apply the strength given you by God to persist in chasing the goal line.

What is your goal line? Is it a goal line to a promotion on a job? Is it a goal line to achieve wealth and riches? Is it a goal line of mental, physical, and spiritual health? Whatever your goal line may be, you must apply the mind God has given you to chase that goal line in your life.

Persistent, applied faith is the theme of this book. It is certainly true that in life you do not get something for nothing. In other words, we cannot expect to get much out of life when we choose to invest so little. It may be true that there are some who have gotten much by doing little, but doing little for much just doesn't add up for the majority of us who desire to be successful. One can be rich through winning the lottery, getting life insurance benefits, or receiving an inheritance, etc., but the word of the wise man proves to be true: "The hand of the diligent maketh rich." One must work at something *diligently* to receive the maximum benefit or satisfaction for his work.

It feels good to have earned a college degree or achieved some other goal into which you have invested many hours of work. The achievement earned becomes very valuable to you. But on the contrary, you feel defeat, resentment, and a lack of assurance if you failed by not persevering long enough or simply by not trying.

As we take this journey in learning the strategies for achieving your dreams, I hope that you will utilize the principles outlined in this book and that you will get the maximum out of your life's dreams and aspirations. You have something that God wants to bring out to be a blessing to the world, and He will be robbed of His glory if you do nothing about it! Now is the time for you to utilize that powerful tool that the Creator has given you — your mind!

You Are a Mind With a Body

When I first read the above statement in the book *Success Through A Positive Attitude*, it really struck me. The truth of this statement was in front of me for many years, and when I began to ponder it, I knew it was true.

"You are a mind with a body!" My physical body does not make choices to live; it only carries out what my mind has chosen for me to do. The same is true for you, my friend. Your body does not have any thinking power; it only carries out the dictates of whatever you have thought in your mind. When I began to realize this truth, it caused me to reevaluate the life choices I had made, why my life was where it was, and how I came to where I am in life.

Usually when we do self-evaluations, we look at the negative things we have done, the mistakes, and so forth, but it is not the purpose of this book for you to look at the past and become discouraged about it. Whatever mistakes and failures you have experienced, you must forgive yourself before you can go on with life and soar above the hurts of the past.

More than that, you must allow God to forgive you. Ask Him to forgive the sins and wrongs of the past, and He will abundantly forgive you and cast them into the sea of His forgetfulness. If He has promised to do this, then why are you scuba diving? You must let go of the past if you are to go on in life. Many cannot go on to higher heights in life because they have allowed the "chicken pen" of the past — some skeleton in the closet, abuse by someone, or their employer unjustly firing them, etc. — to cause feelings of guilt and bitterness to override their desire to forgive. At this point, their dreams become paralyzed, and they cannot go forward to achieve them.

From this point on, I want you to cast away the errors of the past, whether they were committed by you or by some other person who may have offended you. "Cast your burdens upon the Lord," the scripture says. These words of wisdom were penned thousands years ago, because the Creator knew that many could not advance mentally, physically, or spiritually without first letting go of the hurts that were either self-inflicted or inflicted by someone else. Once you have done this, you can fly and go beyond the sky!

The brain is the storehouse of the mind. This brain, the most important organ of the human body, stores the greatest threat to human failure — the human mind. Once one knows the power of the mind and the unlimited possibilities it can conceive, that person will know that whatever a person can conceive in his or her thought processes, they surely can achieve!

The mind is the activity of thought, the electrical process of the brain, where ideas are born. Thoughts are nothing more than things that are tangible to the *mind* but intangible to the *body* in terms of touch and sight. But when applied by faith to whatever enterprise man conceives, the psycho-tangible then becomes physio-tangible.

In other words, what begins in the mind becomes a reality to the sight of man — something he can physically use. This is true of every invention man has created since he first walked upon the earth. Every skyscraper, every car, every house, every piece of clothing that people use, or whatever else that caters to man's needs, began in the thought process of the brain — the mind.

Your Mind Is the Architect

The thought process did not stop there. It then dictated to the body to begin to bring the thought process — the mind's dream — to fruition. As long as it took for the thought process to bring the mind's dream into fruition, then became the visible creation of what the mind conceived — the product. This is what it means that you are a mind with a body.

The *mind* is the architect; the *body* is nothing more that the construction worker of the architect's blueprints. Your mind is the architect and your body serves your mind as the construction worker. What blueprints are you bringing to the table to make changes in your life? Whatever they are, whether you carry them out or not, you have able workers to carry out whatever you conceive in your mind. And as long as you do not violate the laws of the mind, which are the laws of God, there are no limits to what you can achieve.

The Siamese Twins of the Mind

From my reading of the Bible and books dealing with self-help and life achievement, there are two laws that stand out when it comes to life empowerment and achievement. I want to focus on these two laws. Knowing them is half the battle. These two laws are always in operation. They work as Siamese twins.

The first is *the law of compensation.* The Bible says, "Whatsoever a man sows, that shall he also reap." Sow a thought, reap a habit; sow a habit, reap a character; sow a character in life and reap your destiny. This law has been ordained by God in all the affairs of life, and if it is either obeyed or broken, the results will surely be the same.

We see this law in operation every day in the workplace. When I put in my allotted hours of work, on payday I receive compensation in the form of pay. We see this also when it comes to fitness and health. If I consistently exercise, watch what I eat, and get plenty of rest, my compensation will be a fit and healthy body. However, if I neglect to take care of my body and form health-destroying habits that don't keep my body fit, nature compensates, and I'll have poor health.

The moral is that you get out of life what you put into it. If you put in little, you will receive little for compensation. If you put in much, then in some way you will receive much in return.

Garbage in, garbage out. Positive in, positive out. Whatever you sow into your mind, be sure that if that thought is cherished and put into action, you will receive what you put in. That is why it is most important that we put into our minds thoughts that will enrich and edify us so the quality of our lives will be positive, not negative.

I once had a high school friend who could not help but think negatively. I do not know how her life turned out, but I knew back then that my friend would not achieve her life's dreams and goals if she continued to think as she did.

To keep your mind from being negative, you would do well to read the Bible's inspiring promises concerning God's love and His promises of blessing and prosperity. Personalize them for yourself, and repeat these positive thoughts so your mind will be stimulated and kept from becoming negative. Apply Bible principles and watch your life change and your dreams come true. It would also be helpful for you to read inspirational books dealing with positive principles in thought and life.

Our thoughts have much to do with our destinies. If we think negatively, the compensation the mind must obey is the same — negative compensation. And if we conceive and cherish such negative thoughts as hate, greed, murder, and so forth, our mind begins to assimilate them, and we may carry these thoughts out in negative actions which have negative consequences: estrangement from family or friends, distrust of others, imprisonment, or death itself. *Do not underestimate the power of a thought!*

We see the negative side of life on earth every day through the increase of crime, divorce, abuse, and every other negative thing. These things were brought into existence through the power of a thought that led to actions which brought forth results.

On the other hand, when we think on things that are positive, true, lovely, pure, and good, these thoughts have the same effect on the mind as negative thoughts. The body carries these thoughts out into actions, and the compensation is positive, whether it be in good health or pure and virtuous actions.

This is true for life achievements as well. What goals do you have? What do you want to be in life? Whatever you desire to achieve, it is left for you to sow thoughts of success into your human spirit — your mind — and to continually keep them before your mind until they become a part of your psyche. Then it will not be long before your dreams come true, and you will surely begin to fly. The law of compensation has been in operation in your life, giving you exactly what you have put into life, and it has resulted in the life you now enjoy. Utilize the law of compensation positively and watch it compensate you in the achievement of your life's dreams.

The Law of Expectation

Jesus said, "As thou has believed, so be it done unto thee." *The law of expectation* works in equal power to the law of compensation. If you expect something to happen, most likely that thing you expect will compensate you by happening. If you expect poverty, loss, termination of employment, sickness and so forth, sooner or later those things will compensate you by happening.

On the other hand, if you expect health, success, riches or whatever positive thing your mind conceives, the law of compensation will reward you with riches, health and success. Take some time for reflection, and remember the times in your life or in someone else's life when this law of expectation happened as the result of the habitual thoughts or words.

For example, I know someone whose mother passed away while practicing the laws of expectation. For years she talked about how she wanted to die and leave this world. She would pray about it, talk about it, and once at a funeral she stated that she would be the next to die—and indeed, a year later, her expectations came true. She became sick and died!

Her death certificate stated the reason of death — depression. The doctor told her son that his mother had lost the will to live. She willed *not* to live. Her thoughts were so absorbed with death that the biological processes, in obedience to her mind, brought about her final sickness and death.

A more famous example of the law of expectation is seen in the life of the late hip-hop artist Tupac

Shakur. I was reading about his life at the time he starred in the movie "Poetic Justice" with Janet Jackson. The author of the book I was reading quoted a statement Tupac had made that brought chills down my spine. The author related that film director Spike Lee said that although Tupac was an excellent actor then, he believed that in 10 years he would become even greater.

Tupac's reply, according to the author, demonstrated the law of expectation. Tupac predicted that he would be dead in 10 years. Although I've never listened to his music, I've learned that Tupac talked about death a lot in his lyrics, and this has bothered me. It caused me to question why he would write these "semi-prophetic" lyrics. One may never know, but in September 1996, Tupac was shot several times in Las Vegas, Nevada, and eventually died. Was his death a self-fulling prophecy demonstrating the law of compensation along with expectation? I will let the reader decide.

But one thing is certain, if once you sow thoughts in your mind and give expression to them — whether they are negative or positive — you may be sure that the Siamese laws of compensation and expectation will surely give birth and reward you well.

Have a Success Complex

To use these laws correctly to achieve our life's dreams, we must obey them by formulating a "success complex" in our minds. If you think successfully toward a goal or a dream, the body has a way of lining up with your thoughts. It shows in your face, in your walk, and in your talk. Then, as you persevere in your life's goals with a success complex in mind, your life will surely align itself to the complex which you have trained your mind to form. A success complex is nothing more than having a positive mental attitude.

In the Bible, God told Joshua after the death of Moses that if he would obey His commands, Joshua would be assured of success. The same is true for you: If you obey God's commands in the pursuit of your life's dreams, God assures you of positive success in whatever you do. Remember, as long as you do not violate His laws, you can achieve whatever you will. The laws of the mind are the laws of God, stemming from the great law of the universe — the Ten Commandments. You would do well to take the time to read them in Exodus 20:3-17. From them you will learn the foundation of all true life achievement and success.

God has given you a mind to visualize your life's dreams, and He will surely give you the provision to carry them out — but He wants you to do them within the context of His will laid out not only in the Ten Commandments, but also in the words of the Golden Rule: "Do unto others as you would have them do unto you." This eliminates dishonesty in all forms — greed, lying, stealing, cheating etc. — in achieving your life's goals.

No man lives unto himself. There is a wave of influence that ripples very far with everything that we do. Therefore, it is important that you are obedient to the laws of God in carrying out your life's goals, so God can be glorified and mankind can be blessed by your achievements.

Somebody in this world needs to see what God can do for a person who is totally submitted to His will, showing forth God and His love for mankind. This success complex underlies the foundation of all life's achievements.

A common saying is, "Nothing breeds success as much as success." Think about this for a moment: Success breeds its own kind. The mental state of success compensates a person with what he is stating to himself. This is powerful! This is why we must not allow thoughts of failure to enter into our minds.

We were created in the image of God to soar to higher heights. We still have that power! With God making the provision for our vision, there is no such thing as failure! "With God, nothing shall be impossible." No matter who you are, you have the power to choose your destiny for success. You must first think successful thoughts in order to be successful. The salesman who plans to be successful in sales will not be successful if he does not *believe* that he will be successful. If he constantly is thinking about all the rejections he will receive, there is little hope that he will succeed; but if he has the "success complex" of all the sales he is about to have for that day, month, or year, there is no stopping him! Whatever you do, whether in finances, marriage, education, and so forth, if you do not believe that you will be successful, there is little hope that you will be.

Friend, you can fly beyond the sky! Do not allow past personal failures, parental failures, or even the failures of other people to keep you back. *Success is failure turned inside out.* Remember, you are a mind with a body. Your mind has the ability to conceive limitless things. With God in the picture, He will work with you to achieve your life's dreams.

If Michael Jordan would have allowed the "failure" of being cut from the high school varsity basketball tryouts limit and destroy his dream of one day making it in professional basketball, the world would never have seen the greatest player in basketball accomplish so much.

Some of us have allowed our dreams to become shattered because of events we thought of as failures. You are not a failure if you have conceived something and have done your best to achieve it, but it didn't work out. Maybe you miscalculated something which would have been successful with a little more time or training. If at first you do not succeed, try, try again!

The Turn of a Screw

Alexander Graham Bell was the patented inventor of the telephone. Many others had claimed to have invented the telephone, but the Supreme Court named Bell as the inventor. Why? You will see when you read his story.

Phillip Reis was considered to be the person who apparently came close to success, but the thing that stopped him from being the inventor of the telephone was the turn of a screw! Reis was at the brink of that fortune-making invention, but he could not figure out how to transmit sound waves into uninterrupted sound current.

The U. S. Supreme Court noted that "...Reis knew what had to be done in order to transmit speech by electricity is very apparent, for in his first paper he said: 'As soon as it is possible to produce, anywhere and in any manner, vibrations whose curves shall be the same as those of any given tone or combination of tones, we shall receive the same impression as that tone or combination of tones would have produced on us...'"

Reis discovered how to reproduce musical tones, but he did no more. He could *sing* through his apparatus, but he could not *talk* through it. He conceded this. Reis was at the point of a breakthrough, but he could not figure out how to step over the line.

In the book *Success With A Positive Mental Attitude*, W. Clement Stone noted concerning Bell and the telephone, "As in the case of the Wright brothers, the something more Bell added was comparatively simple. He switched from an intermittent to a continuous current, the only type capable of reproducing human speech. The two currents are exactly the same direct current. 'Intermittent' means breaking with a slight pause. Specifically, Bell kept the circuit open instead of breaking the circuit intermittently as Reis had done."

Because of this, the Supreme Court concluded about the invention of the telephone: "Reis never thought of it, and he failed to transmit speech telegraphically. Bell did, and he succeeded. Under such circumstances it is impossible to hold that what Reis did was an anticipation of the discovery of Bell. To follow Reis is to fail, but to follow Bell is to succeed. The difference between the two is just the difference between failure and success. If Reis had kept on he might have found out the way to succeed, but he stopped and failed. Bell took up his work and carried it on to a successful result."

Friend, whose example will you follow? Will you give up, as did Reis, and allow a Bell in your life to take up where you left off and finally succeed and carry out your dream? All you have to do is to turn the screw. If you were Reis, how would you feel? Life achievement is not for quitters. Don't quit. No matter how it looks, do not quit on your dreams and goals. Keep on keeping on! Pray, believe, and work until God taps you on the shoulder and tells you, "You can stop now." Do not quit!

This story of the invention of the telephone by Bell is an assurance that success is 90 percent perseverance. Do not forget that. It reminds me of the shortest speech made in human history that still has a powerful impact today. Winston Churchill made a seven-word speech to his countrymen in England during World War II that encouraged them to get past so-called failures in the war of life. Churchill said, "Never, never, never, never, never give up!," and after he said those words, he sat down. What I'm saying to you is never, never, never, never, never give up! *You are just a step away from achieving you life's dreams!*

It all begins and ends with how you think. It is up to you what you choose to think about, but one thing is certain: Do not expect to achieve your dreams and fly — and fail to put forth the necessary effort of bringing it to pass — if you do not believe that by God's grace you can bring it to pass. God helps those who help themselves.

I would now like to share with you my personal philosophy of success when it comes to life achievement. I believe that in our quest for life achievement, it would be good for each of us to formulate a philosophy of life so we may have a guide to help us reach our goals.

My Philosophy on Life Achievement

First, *success without God is failure.* You can achieve all you want to, but without God in the picture, the most glamorous success in the world amounts to failure. All of us will have to stand before our Maker and give an account of the life we have lived. We do not belong to ourselves; we belong to God, the One who made us.

We have been given a lease on life, and He expects us to make the most of it! He sent His Son, Jesus Christ, to die for our sins; and by confession of our sins and faith toward Him by loving obedience to His will, we will be saved and make heaven our eternal home. To leave out the One who has given each of us the power to get wealth and success is to fail miserably. We must put God first, last, and best in everything we do in life.

Second is the truth that *God wants me to be prosperous.* The Bible says, "I wish above all things, that thou mayest prosper and be in health even as thy soul prospereth." These words came from the mind of God. And since they came from His mind, I must choose to allow His thoughts of success and prosperity to be mine. Therefore, I am not hindered or ashamed in achieving my heart's desires.

Third, *I am created in the image of God.* Because of this truth, I know that I have the God-given ability to direct my thoughts and emotions and to ordain my destiny. And that is why I believe I can fly beyond the sky.

Fourth, *I can be truly successful in all that I do only by obeying God laws.* God's mental, physical, and spiritual laws were written with my well-being in mind. They were given to keep me from experiencing failure in this life and in the life to come . Therefore, I lovingly obey them for the fulfillment of my life's dreams, knowing that the laws of expectation and compensation will surely follow me all the days of my life.

Last, *I believe in prayer and in the miraculous answers that it brings.* I have seen God change circumstances in my life around to where I knew that it was God who did it. He has given me the desires of my heart, and I know that by applying the power of prayer I can receive and achieve all things. Friend, what is your personal philosophy? When you make up your mind that you can fly beyond the sky, you can then exercise the power of faith.

Strategy #2
Exercise the Power of Faith

No one can underestimate the power of faith in achieving our life's goals. Faith was given to us by our Creator to exercise in all our daily enterprises. This element of faith is so important that without it, the world would not function. Everything we do, we do by faith. Faith believes in the inevitable.

For example, we go to bed at night believing that we are going to get up in the morning. When we get out of bed, we believe that our legs will have the strength to buoy us up and give our body the support that it needs to walk. We believe that when we get into our vehicles, they will start when we turn on the ignition.

Faith underlies everything we do. At first we do not see results, but by faith we believe that the results we desire will come to pass. So if you will apply the power of faith to achieve your life's dreams, there is no stopping you.

You Have What It Takes

The Bible teaches that God "..has dealt to every man the measure of faith." This is good news, because God has put the potential in all of us to succeed by the mere fact that He has given us the gift of faith. *You have what it takes to succeed!* You must believe this. God has given you the power to succeed to any heights of human achievement because He has implanted this within you! This faith is the power of belief. You have unlimited potential because of the faith that you have within you. But you must exercise it in order to receive the benefits that come by exercising faith.

Mahatma Gandhi once said, "Man often becomes what he believes himself to be. If I have the belief that I can do it, I shall have the capacity to do it even if I may not have it at the beginning." This is a very powerful point. You may not have it now, but if you continue to believe the inevitable, the law of compensation will reward you with results. Do you have faith? Believing that you can accomplish something makes the journey toward achieving your life's goals a lot easier.

What Faith Can Do

The Bible defines faith as the "..substance of things hoped for, the evidence of things not seen." Although you do not see the tangible results of your dreams and aspirations, by the power of faith you see them tangibly in your mind. Then, by applying efforts in proportion to your faith, the results you desire come to pass.

What am I saying? I am saying that you have an idea that can bring you above want and poverty. You have an idea that will give you the power to reach your dreams and potential. Your idea is a seed, needing only to be watered by the power of faith. Then it will blossom into the fruit of wealth, riches, and advancement in the field of your lifework. You must first have the vision, and then God will make the provision! "If God be for you, who can be against you?" When you exercise faith, God will give you the wisdom and power to persevere and to bring your dreams to pass.

African-Americans in the 20th century dreamed of a day when they would be treated as equals. The reality before them was the Jim Crow laws, which dealt with segregated seating in movies, restaurants, and buses. Segregation was the order of the day; furthermore, the term "separate but equal" did not grant the equality blacks knew was rightfully theirs. Faith inspired and enabled millions of African-Americans to fight for their civil rights in the 1950s and '60s to achieve the same civil freedom and the same rights as their white counterparts.

When they became tired of being sick and tired, they stood up and worked for what was rightfully theirs until they achieved the freedoms they desired. This achievement was made possible by having a dream, believing in the rightness of the dream, and putting into action the necessary steps that it would take to bring civil freedom to blacks.

Yes, there was much opposition, tragedies, and setbacks to their dream of civil equality, but they persevered. Marjorie Margolies-Mezvinsky, a former member of the U. S. House of Representatives, said, "You have to be prepared to lose before you can win." What if they had given up? What if they had believed that the dream was impossible? The answer is simple: They would have remained in the same condition they were in before they began to fight. They would have remained "in their place," and they would have sunk lower into the pit of segregated oppression. Time that they could have used in attaining their dream of civil rights would have been time they remained as second-class citizens.

You must not stand still and allow time to fly by! Time does not wait for anyone. It's like a car speeding past pedestrians without a care about who they are. So does time pass by all men without regard to their race, religion, color, or status in life. It's up to you right now to decide to get up and take action. Without faith you will not see the need to take action. There may be some setbacks, but with faith conceived and persistently applied, positive results will happen in your life.

The Power of Faith Realized

I love the story I read in the book *Think and Grow Rich: A Black Choice* by Dr. Dennis Kimbro. I want to relate this story to you to show you what faith can do in the lives of those who mean business in rising above their unwanted conditions.

Only 18 cents and two cans of sardines separated this young man from poverty and starvation. At this time, he moved from one cheap apartment to another in search of a home and a dream.

After spending 20 years in the military, he had fallen in love with writing. Little did this man know that his literary talent would someday bring him fame and fortune. Notice that I noted that fame and fortune met him later. Like a lot of things in life, writing did not come to him easily.

His income was erratic and sparse, and it seemed like his bills never failed to arrive on time. Although he was offered several 9-to-5 jobs which would have released him from want and poverty, he turned them all down, because in his heart his faith told him, "I am a writer, and I have to keep writing". A writer he was, and writing he did.

Determined to succeed as a writer, he kept on with his dream, and then he came up with an idea. He had the faith to believe that it could be done, and he applied his faith by going after his heart's desire. He figured that it would take about three years or so to write the project he had in mind. Indeed, it did take him three years — plus nine more! It took him a total of 12 years, and brought him to the brink of bankruptcy, both financial and spiritual.

He spent more than 6,500 hours of research in 57 libraries, traveling throughout the United States, over to London, on to West Africa, and to many places in search of his dream. His travel expenses totaled more than $30,000. After nine years, this man in search of a dream was more than $100,000 in debt.

This would have kept many of us from pursuing our dreams any further, but thank God, this man believed. Although he kept persevering, the story goes on to say that he was at his wit's end, and he even contemplated suicide. But at the moment he was ready to kill himself, it seemed as if God had stopped him.

At his lowest point, it seemed like giving up was the only thing to do. He was discouraged by the ridicule of his family and friends, by the many setbacks he had experienced, and probably by a threatening disbelief in his own sincerity and the power of his dream. But then he met his greatest source of power — applied faith — and his life turned around.

Alex Haley, the man who had this dream, said, "Recognizing, perhaps for the first time in my life the amazing power of an enduring faith, I carefully surveyed my bleak circumstances to determine just how much of this form of riches I possessed. The assessment was both revealing and gratifying."

This revelation caused Haley to dismiss all thoughts of killing himself. His best-seller, *Roots*, made him a millionaire, and in the words of Dr. Kimbro, "Since 1977 — for his faith — Haley has been honored by more than 400 different countries, institutions and organizations. For his faith, Haley has become one of the most celebrated writers ever, winning a Pulitzer Prize in the process. For his faith, "Roots," the television series, broke all viewing records and seized nine Emmys, becoming reportedly the highest-rated television show ever. Since then, Alex Haley has passed away, but his works haven't. His works surely follow him.

From reading this story, I hope you can see what faith can do for a man who means business. Haley made the following comment about his efforts, and I hope it will inspire you as it inspired me: "The only way to succeed is through hard, hard work and plenty of faith." What more can be said?

Haley's story stands out in my mind from all the success stories I have read, for here was a man who gave all he had. He could have turned back many of times, but he kept on with his dream. He persevered until he achieved his heart's desire.

Friend, it can be the same for you. No matter what you desire to achieve in life, you must believe it can be done. With faith as the foundation, you must diligently work hard to achieve your goals. There is no substitute for hard work.

Terrie Williams, a public relations agent in New York, said, "Whatever your plans and goals, you must honestly look into yourself and know that you will give all that it takes to reach your objectives. You don't get anything in life without taking a chance." Taking a chance is what it is going to take.

Do Not Be Afraid To Take a Chance

Faith takes chances! If it didn't, it wouldn't be faith. When a couple gets married, they take a chance at love, not knowing where their relationship will be in five, 10, or 20 years. They believe they are doing the right thing, and they take a step of faith in tying the knot. Yes, marriages do fail, and separation and divorce do result, but at the altar that is the last thing in the couple's minds.

How is it with you? What goals do you aspire to? What visions of success do you imagine? Whatever your goal or vision is, if you believe it can be done, you must take a chance in achieving what you believe for. Faith does not take into account whether or not our dream will fail. Our dream may take some time to come into fruition, but as the Bible says, "Hope deferred is as a tree of life when it comes." When it comes to pass, you can look back at the effort it took for you to get there and have the satisfaction of knowing that the struggle is all over. From this experience, you learn wisdom that you can pass on to others who desire to reach their life's dreams.

When you refuse to take a chance, you are imprisoning yourself and limiting the power of faith. God has put faith within you, and it is only waiting to be released by your consent. You are as the eagle in the chicken pen, not realizing his power and potential.

Patrice Gaines, a reporter for the Washington Post, said, "The greatest imprisonment of all, and therefore, the greatest freedom, too, is in your mind." Your bondage or freedom is up to you! How are you going to use the power of faith to reach the goals that you are about to launch into? It's up to you how high you want to go in life. You have the choice to flee as a bird from the cage of unbelief, doubt, and procrastination or to remain in that cage. Your faith, coupled with God's power, is the force that will free you.

Believe and you *shall* receive. Stop wishing and start *doing*. "The difference between a goal and a wish is: a wish you never do anything about; a goal you do something about ," said John Raye. You can wish until the sky falls upon Chicken Little's head, but it does nothing for you until you do something about it.

Clint Eastwood said, "Figure what you want out of life, then set your goals and maintain them as long as it is biologically possible." Jesus said, "According to your faith, be it unto you." Keep these words before your mind as you seek to change your life and soar to higher heights. Whatever you believe, when it is applied with hard work, it will come to pass. You have only to believe.

Have Faith in God And in the Power of Prayer

True faith is centered on a belief in God. Since faith is a gift that comes from God, it must be harnessed and applied to the principles outlined in scripture. Jesus told Peter, "Have faith in God." He told Peter this when it came to moving mountains out of the way and casting them into the sea. When you aspire to achieve your life's dream, there are some fundamentals you must use to receive what you desire.

The power of prayer — Prayer is a heaven-ordained means to get closer to God and expect great things from Him. Often many us do not pray, because the outlook seems hopeless, but if you commit your dreams and aspirations to God, nothing is impossible! Go to God, commit yourself to pray, and ask Him to lead and guide you in the pursuit of your dreams. Ask for His will to be carried out or adjusted, according to His infinite wisdom. God sees the end from the beginning. You can safely trust Him to give you your heart's desire. Wait for Him to answer. He will often answer you by inspiring your thoughts and giving you the wisdom of exactly what to do and how to do it. Then ask Him to give you the strength to carry out His plan for your life.

Your prayer can go something like this: "Heavenly Father, I come to You, thanking You for the power You have given me to fulfill my life's dream. I ask you in the Name of Jesus to give me the wisdom and strength to carry out my life's dream. Bless it so You can receive the glory and the honor, Amen."

This example is a model to show you how to come to God for the fulfillment of your heart's desires. The Bible says, "Delight thyself in the Lord and he shall give thee the desires of thy heart." When you commit your ways to God and it is His will for you to succeed, you are on the road to higher heights!

Persistent effort — Work until the things you have dreamed of and prayed for become a reality. Remember Alex Haley's story? He could have given up long before he had his breakthrough, but he persevered until the blessing came. God often allows us to go through such experiences for us to appreciate the blessings we seek when it comes to fulfilling our life's dreams. He could rain these blessings down upon us as soon as we ask, but in His infinite wisdom he has given us brain, bone, and muscle to think, pray, and execute until our dreams become a reality.

This reminds me of the story of one of the world's greatest inventors, Thomas Edison. Having had only a few years of formal education, Edison became the inventor of the light bulb and many other inventions—after 10,000 failures! Many of us have never tried even once to achieve something. We complain because race, poverty, bad luck, and other things are holding us back. Yet we haven't taken the first step of faith that, if consistently applied, would raise us up beyond want and would take us up the hill of success we desire. The example of Thomas Edison should put to silence our excuses for not achieving our dreams.

You Have the Power To Create Your Destiny

Persistence is faith in practice. That's right — persistence is the power of faith in practice. It has been proven over and over again in the lives of achievers the world over. They believed in their vision, and they worked at that vision until it became a reality.

It reminds me of the story in Genesis chapters 1 and 2 about the first entrepreneurial project. God was the first entrepreneur. He had a faith vision in mind! He wanted to create a world to reflect His glory, and He wanted to create beings that would love and serve Him in return. This vision began in His mind. Then He applied His vision and brought to pass that which He visualized.

Friend, you and I were created with that same power! Not in the sense that we can create a physical world as planet Earth, but we have the power to create our destinies! It begins in the mind, and then we bring forth the action, thereby bringing it into existence.

Wally "Famous" Amos once said, "It is your mental attitude which creates results in your life." How true this is! I would like to take this a step further. Your mental attitude in application is what creates results in your life. Wishful thinking never made one rich; neither will it make you successful in your life's dreams without applying some practical faith.

The story is told of a salesman working on a winter day, trying to sell insurance from business to business. He did not make any sales. When he returned to his office, he told one of the executives, "You wait and see. I am going to go back to those same prospects and sell more insurance than all of you guys combined."

Indeed, this salesman went back to all of the businesses where he had attempted to sell insurance before and sold 66 new contracts! This is faith applied. The salesman first believed that he could do it, then he worked and persevered until his faith became a reality! Friend, your faith can become a reality, too. You only have to believe and continue to believe until you receive your heart's desire. Prayer applied to a working faith will guarantee success in whatever field you aspire to.

Change How You Think

The principles discussed so far are all well and good to those who have a positive mental attitude, but it would be an injustice to assume that all who read this material have the attitude it takes to make their dreams come true.

Faith is nothing more that a positive mental attitude conceived and applied in your life endeavors. However, there are many who have allowed the cobwebs of negativity to possess their minds. They do not achieve because they choose to believe that they cannot achieve. They allow many things to keep them from succeeding. We can name 1,001 things that hinder people from succeeding, but if we could break it down to one thing, it is a *negative mental attitude*. One thing is for certain: You will never achieve your goals and dreams with a negative mental attitude. If you have this attitude, you must eliminate it before you can utilize your God-given faith. In other words, you must change how you think.

A lack of self-confidence is a major reason for negative thinking. Low self -worth has damaged millions who otherwise might have risen to any height they desired through self-confidence centered in God.

A person must get into his mind that he is someone because he was "fearfully and wonderfully made" in the image of God to reflect and glorify Him. *Self-worth is gained only by an intimate relationship with God.* The self-confidence a person gains is based on the knowledge that God has given him abilities and gifts that, if exercised by faith and divine guidance, will-help him to achieve the heights of faith he desires. His self-confidence grows by the exercise of faith in his daily struggle to attain his goals and dreams.

If you lack confidence to succeed, you need not despair. God will grant you the faith you need, not only in His ability to empower you but also to believe that through Him you can! There is no need for anyone to feel inferior and unsuccessful because of the circumstances that surround him and have shaped his life.

Many people would not be able to ride a horse if the horse only knew how much power he has! Life would not ride many people if they only knew the power they have to shake off the saddle of hard knocks. Change your thoughts! The mind can only hold one thought at a time. If you struggle to maintain positive thoughts, pray that God will give you the strength to think positively, and practice the law of mental substitution by placing a positive thought in the place of a negative one.

This is good for those who are addicted to bad habits. The thought of the bad habit must come to the mind before the body responds by carrying out the impulses of the mind. "Without me ye can do nothing," said Jesus. When the bad thought comes to your mind, look to heaven for grace and strength. Then apply the law of substitution, and by the grace of God you are strengthening your mental powers and thinking positive thoughts. As your thoughts are habitually positive, you will lean toward these positive thoughts.

Change Your Words

Words are the written and verbal expressions of the mind. In human communication, whatever the mind thinks, it expresses in written or verbal words. It is interesting to note that words have power to change how you feel. That's why people are moved by hearing Dr. Martin Luther King give his "I Have a Dream" speech; by listening to John F. Kennedy talking about what one person can do for an entire nation; or by enjoying a favorite song sung by a famous musical artist.

The specific words we speak and the words we use control the way we think. Words have power to persuade others as well as yourself! How would you feel if you told yourself that you were stupid or ugly? These words react upon your beliefs about your intelligence and personal appearance. Feelings of inferiority would arise, and, if repeated in thought or word, they would eventually affect how you think and live.

But when you understand that you are a *masterpiece* of God's creation, and you say to yourself, "I am fearfully and wonderfully made intellectually and in appearance," how would that affect you? Of course, your mind-set and your life would change. If you believed these words, continually thought on them, and verbalized them, they would definitely control both your thoughts and actions.

If you happen to be in an "unfortunate" situation, this book is not telling you to deny the reality of your situation. Instead, learn to deal with it in a positive way en route to rising above it. Thus, your faith will rise above your circumstances, and you will fly beyond the sky.

If you were a salesperson, instead of saying, "Everybody is *not* going to buy from me," say, "Somebody is going to say yes!" Notice, you are not denying the fact that someone may say no, but you are speaking in the affirmative. You are stating that though you will have some no's, someone will be sure to say yes. This makes a lot of difference. This will give you the power to persevere.

Do you believe that Colonel Sanders would have died rich if he had thought for one moment that no one would say yes to his recipe after hearing hundreds of no's? You be the judge.

You can change the climate of your *words* just by changing the climate of your *thoughts*. Instead of saying, "I feel good," you can say, "I feel fantastic," "I feel phenomenal," or "I feel incredible!" Say these words to yourself with emotion and feeling in front of a mirror and see how you feel. Make new choices of words as you verbalize your faith.

Below is an example of changing good words into empowering words that can affect your life for the better.

Old Boring Words	*Newly Formed Exciting Words*
Good	Amazing
Well	Unstoppable

Tasty	Fabulous
Fast	Explosive
Lucky	Incredibly blessed
I can achieve my dreams	I will achieve my dreams
I won!	I am a world champion!
Things are going well	It doesn't get as good as this!
You can do it	You're as good as it gets!

Protect Your Dreams

Thousands of thoughts come to your mind on a daily basis, but it is up to you which thoughts you allow to reside in your mind. You cannot stop birds from flying over your head, but you certainly can keep them from building a nest on your head! Protect your mind as you would protect your wallet!

If you knew there were pickpockets around and you realized the potential danger, you would exercise the greatest care to assure that no one came close enough to steal your wallet.

You may not agree, but many do not protect their minds from people stealing their dreams! Many a dream has been stolen by individuals who were jealous of that dream. They instilled doubt, unbelief, and outright hostility into what you desired. You have exposed the "wallet"of your mind only to allow another to instill negativity in your mind, thereby stealing your dream. Sometimes — maybe most of the time — it would be better to keep things to yourself and not to relate your dreams too early!

It reminds me of a relative whose "religion" in life is to keep everything a secret from everybody. It was puzzling to me at first, but life's experiences have taught me the wisdom of that "religion." It is not always best to tell others your dreams and aspirations; especially those who desire something better for themselves. Be selective with whom you share your dreams! They may instill doubt in you, or worse yet, they may steal your dream and say it was their own!

It is like the housewife who loves to cook and innocently relates to one of her girlfriends the secret ingredient in a recipe. But that "friend" takes the secret recipe, patents it, puts it on the market, makes her millions — and then spreads the story about how *she* invented that recipe. Funny? It happens more than you think.

So protect your mind, and protect your dreams! They are the greatest asset you have. You can dream big, and with applied and verbalized faith you can achieve big. It's all up to you. With the power of faith, you will surely succeed in speaking your dreams into existence!

Strategy #3
Speaking Your Dreams Into Existence
(The Power of Prophetic Suggestion)

Thou shalt also decree a thing, and it shall be established unto thee....

Job 22:28

By utilizing the power of faith, you can prophesy your dreams into existence! This chapter could be a companion chapter on the power of faith, but in this chapter you will learn about the power of prophetic suggestion. This is an exciting discovery!

Speaking your dreams into existence is the power of faith verbalized. Knowing the power of thought is key, but speaking what you desire to come to pass is even more powerful! Spoken words are nothing more than your thoughts verbalized. When the question is asked, "What's on your mind?," you are simply being asked to verbalize your thoughts.

This truth is important, because with prophetic suggestion, you plant the seeds of faith into your mind, affecting your life and giving you the mental fuel to persevere in making your dreams come true.

E. G. White, an inspirational author, brought out this truth perfectly by stating, "It is a law of nature that our thoughts and feelings are encouraged and strengthened as we give them utterance. While words express thoughts, it is also true that thoughts follow words."

This has proven true in our lives. You may have heard the saying, "Be careful of what you pray for." This is true, because you do not know what may happen. This is also true of the words that you speak. We have used this power of suggestion without even knowing the power behind it. We have heard a parent say to a child, "You're just like your father"; or "You're just like your mother. They didn't accomplish anything, and neither will you!" The power of prophetic suggestion operated from the time these words were uttered.

Many a child's destiny was determined by the "prophecies" that parents, friends, and relatives placed on them by verbalizing thoughts of destruction and poverty. It may not be able to be explained, but this fact is true: "Life and death are in the power of the tongue." You have the ability to bless or curse your life and the lives of others by the words you speak. It would be a word to the wise to guard your words. What you utter can become a self-fulfilling prophecy!

The story is told of a young man who returned home from work wearing muddy shoes. When he got home, instead of taking off his muddy shoes on the porch, he entered the house, muddying the carpet. His mother had previously warned him about not entering the house with muddy shoes. An argument ensued between the mother and the son.

In frustration, the mother uttered these words: "Son, if you're not going to listen to me, the day will come when you will not be able to use your feet again." The son walked out of the house in anger and left to go to the bank to cash his check. On his way home, he cut through an alley and encountered a robber. The robber commanded the young man to give him his money and to turn around.

The young man did as he was ordered, and suddenly two shots rang out. The robber shot the young man in his back, paralyzing him from the waist down, and to this day he is paralyzed, never to walk again. What made this happen? It was the prophetic words of his mother! The young man, enraged at what happened, did not speak to his mother for two years. He knew that what his mother uttered came to pass!

What made this so interesting is that the same mother prophesied over her younger son shortly after this incident, but this time there was a different result. In this case, the younger son was giving his mother trouble. He was arguing with her while waiting for some friends to pick him up. As he was leaving, the mother in all innocence said that if he continued to be disobedient, he would wind up going to jail. Not paying any attention to his mother, he entered the vehicle and drove off with his friends. Minutes after he left, the car in which he was a passenger was stopped by the city police. Unbeknown to this younger son, the car he was in was stolen, and the police had been looking for it.

The young man and the driver were apprehended, arrested on certain charges, and sent to jail. Due to the fact that the younger son was at the wrong place at the wrong time, he was sent to boot camp for two years.

What caused this to happen? Was it simply bad luck? I believe it was because of the prophetic utterances their mother had made! The mother in these two instances did not *purposely* prophesy calamity to come on her sons, but what she uttered did come to pass, whether she expected it to happen or not.

If you have the power to utter your destiny without thinking seriously about what you're saying, how much more powerful will you be when you utter words that come to pass in the fulfillment of your dreams!

In Genesis, we see the Creator speaking this world into existence. God said, "Let there be light: and there was light"(Genesis 1:3). When God spoke, things happened! We are created with that same power—not in the sense that we are divine and can create a physical world as God did; rather, we have the power to create our destinies by the words we utter.

There is a story in the Bible about a man named Jacob. He married a woman named Rachel, whom he loved dearly. According to scripture, Jacob prophesied his wife's death unknowingly. When confronted by his father-in-law about some stolen goods, Jacob denied that he had stolen them. Jacob added that whoever had stolen his father-in-law's goods would die. Little did Jacob know that his dear wife was the culprit!

Several chapters later, the Bible records that while giving birth to Jacob's last son, Rachel died. What caused it? Was it the complications of childbirth? No, it was the prophetic words of death that came from the mouth of Jacob that caused his wife's death!

This power of prophetic speech can be shown over and over again in the Bible, and not just there, but in life today. Your words have the power to bring about the results which you speak. Don't misunderstand me for saying that we all are prophets in the sense of foretelling the future. What I am saying is that the constructive or destructive words we utter have the power to influence our lives, causing the desired result to happen, whether good or bad.

You are what you speak. If you think and speak *negative* things, nature will align itself to what you speak, thereby bringing it to pass. But if you utter *positive* things, nature will work in your life the same as if you had spoken negative things. This power of prophetic suggestion is a dangerous tool in your life if you do not use it right. But when correctly used, it can become a power for the person who desires success in any area of life.

As you prophesy your thoughts, you will encourage and strengthen yourself as you achieve your dreams. It is like a football or basketball team pumping themselves up before a game. This pumping-up session is often used to enthuse the players into better action. You are playing the game of life. You have only one chance to win. There will be no overtime period to perform if you do not win in regulation time. You must win; you must succeed — and with God's help you will!

Prophetic suggestion utilizes the truths you have learned in the previous chapters to pump you up into a state of belief and confidence, inducing you to act successfully. Prophetic suggestion is a different method of suggestion from what is commonly termed auto-suggestion or self-suggestion, which is simply the communication between the conscious and the subconscious minds, where thoughts and principles are instilled.

An experiment was done at a church, where a woman who was only about five feet tall asked a tall, strong man to come to the front. Showing how the power of prophetic suggestion works, she told the man to stick out his arm and utter three times, "I am a wonderful person." This he did, and when the young woman attempted to bring his arm down, she was unable to do so.

Then she asked the strong man to utter three more words. This time the words were negative affirmations: "I am a terrible person." When the young woman attempted to pull down the strong man's arm this time, she did it with ease. The results of this experiment were so amazing, the whole assembly was shocked.

This again shows that the words you utter have power in them to affect you for better or for worse. What words are you saying about yourself? What words are you allowing people to say about you? Many have allowed the negative "prophecies" of others to affect their lives in such a powerful way, they have fulfilled them in their lives.

My message to you is: Do not allow yourself or anyone else to utter future failure over you in any way! Do not allow such words to become a part of you. Rescind those words in the Name of Jesus, and they will not come to pass. Prophetic suggestion is to be used in a positive way to strengthen your belief in the accomplishment of your life's dreams and goals. Therefore speak into existence that which you desire.

Prophetic suggestion is the communication that comes from the result of the power of faith speaking or prophesying the desires of your heart into existence. Prophetic suggestion verbalizes the power of faith into your life, influencing and reacting on the mind of the person. This is similar to self-suggestion, but the difference is that prophetic suggestion is centered in God, thereby affirming by the power of speech what God is going to bring to pass in your life.

When you commit your life's dreams and goals to God, you give Him the permission to become a partner in your enterprises for life achievement. When you utilize the power of faith, backed by much prayer for your life's dreams, you can then prophesy your dreams into existence.

E. G. White again noted, "The more you talk faith, the more faith you will have. The more you dwell upon discouragements, talking to others about your trials, and enlarging upon them to enlist the sympathy which you crave, the more discouragements and trials you will have."

Prophesy your dreams in the face of your discouragement! Prophesy into existence achieving your goals! As you verbalize these thoughts of successful achievement, your mind will adapt itself to what you are saying. Your words will become a part of your subconscious mind. Words spoken not only have the potential to affect those who hear, but to affect the speaker himself.

By the power of speech, the words spoken affect the mind of the speaker, thereby affecting his actions. If you habitually tell lies, sooner or later you will begin to believe your own lies. Many believe their own lies every day! The thought that you cannot achieve your life's dreams is a lie that many believe on a daily basis. You can reverse this trend in your life if you will simply follow these simple instructions on prophesying your destiny.

Helpful Suggestions

One of things you can do is read the Bible and its precious promises of achievement. Here are a few scriptures that you can utilize when you speak your dreams into existence:

For as he [a man] **thinketh in his heart, so is he...**

Proverbs 23:7

> If thou canst believe, all things are possible to him that believeth.
>
> **Mark 9:23**

> Lord I believe: help thou mine unbelief.
>
> **Mark 9:24**

> ...whosoever shall say unto this mountain, Be thou removed, and be thou cast into the sea; and shall not doubt in his heart, but shall believe that those things which he saith shall come to pass; he shall have whatsoever he saith.
>
> **Mark 11:23**
>
> [my favorite scripture on prophetic suggestion.]

> ...According to your faith be it unto you.
>
> **Matthew 9:29.**

> ...faith without works is dead.
>
> **James 2:20.**

> ...What things soever ye desire, when ye pray, believe that ye receive them, and ye shall have them.
>
> **Mark 11:24**

Read these scriptures, memorize them, and take these promises of success into your marriage, business, dreams, and goals. Pray to God for miracles to happen, and then utter your faith by saying, "By the grace of God, I will have _____ by such-and-such a time. By the grace of God, I am losing the weight I desire. By the grace of God, I am achieving my life's dreams."

Speak those things that are not as though they were! The Bible is packed with promises that anyone can utilize as long as they put God first, last, and best in their goals. Each scripture promise is likened to an acorn. Using microscopes, scientists have discovered that centered in each acorn is an oak tree. In each promise given in the Bible, the "oak tree"of your dream, goal, or aspiration is centered.

If you claim and utter these promises, the seed of your goal or aspiration will begin to breed life, germinating into the tree of achievement you desire! Does that sound like fun? Knowing this truth has made the power of faith, prayer and prophetic suggestion even more exciting. After you have committed yourself to prayer and to claim the promises of the Bible, speak and affirm what is already yours.

In Old Testament times, God spoke these words of prophecy to a man named Abraham, whose wife was barren: "I have made thee a father of many nations." God spoke this to a man who did not have even *one* child! God spoke as if a large nation of people were already in existence. This is the power of prophetic suggestion! Speak as if your goal or dream were actually yours! It will do wonders for your thinking.

If you are poor and desire to be rich, prophetically utter: "I am rich; I am a millionaire.." If you are sick and cannot get well, say: "I am feeling much better." If you aspire to excel in school, work, or some other enterprise, say: "I am successful in my field." Speak as if your goal were already attained, and watch miracles happen! If you have to utter your desires 50 times a day to yourself to bring your dreams into existence, do it without delay. Believe me, your thinking will change, and so will your life!

A Prophetic Letter

Another thing you can do is to write a letter to yourself; a written prophecy of success and achievement. This will deepen the impression you feed into your subconscious mind, thereby affecting your life.

Whatever you aspire to, you must have a plan in order for your vision to be carried out.

Wishful thinking did not build the city of New York! A plan was first prepared and then carried out. Although you have your dreams by prophetic utterance, you must plan on how you will bring your heart's desire to pass. A prophetic letter serves as a plan, but it is also a faith-filled prediction of your achieving your life's dreams. Your prophetic letter can read something like this:

"By the first of day of January 20_____, I will have my dream fulfilled in the form of _____. I will render the following service or exertions in the pursuit of my already fulfilled dream. I will _____ backed by the power of faith and prayer so that my dream will come true. I will render constant thanks to God for my dream being fulfilled. I will not allow any negative thoughts of failure or defeat come between me and my dream. I am successful because God has made me successful.

"While I am doing my part, I know that God is doing His part in bringing my dream to pass. Therefore, I will prophetically utter, 'I have my dream; I am successful; I am_____; I am already _____.' By the grace of God, these words that I am saying are true, and therefore are in existence. Although my dream is not in physical fulfillment, it is already fulfilled by the words of my mouth."

Signed,
Your name

Speak Confidently

Repeat these words to yourself after you have prayed to God to bring your dream to pass. Repeat this prophetic letter every morning and evening. Do it every day until you have memorized your letter of achievement and it will become a part of you.

By following these instructions of prophetic suggestion, you are expressing God-given faith in the pursuit of your dreams. And by doing this, you are influencing yourself to believe that by the grace of God your dream is fulfilled and is in the process of fulfillment! God operates in response to your faith, and by prophetically uttering your heart's desire and putting forth the effort, you give Him the opportunity to bring your dreams to pass. Speak confidently, and watch the power of the Almighty bring your dreams to pass!

Concentrate on your utterances and, when you repeat them, do it with feeling. This stimulates the mind to more readily adapt itself to what you're saying. Speak as if you know that what you are saying will come to pass. Do not forget to add God into the equation. So often man often looks to himself as the answer to all his problems and depends upon himself, but the truth is that man cannot solve his problems in life without the help of God.

He is the One who brought you into existence. He is the One who gives you air to breathe, which you need every second of the day to survive. He is One who has given you the power to get wealth. He is the One who provides the sun and the rain, causing crops to grow to sustain life. Finally, God is the One who has given you that powerful mind to exercise in achieving your life's dreams. If God were to stop His constant, watchful care over the affairs of your life, you would go nowhere in your life's dreams. You would cease to exist!

It is true that a person can succeed in life without acknowledging God in the equation. He has given all of us the power to acknowledge Him or not to acknowledge Him. In spite of the fact that many do not acknowledge Him, He still gives them the strength and power to acquire their heart's desires.

The purpose of this book is not for you to look to yourself as the source of life empowerment in achieving your dreams; the purpose of this book is to lead you to the One who has given you the power to achieve success — God. To acknowledge Him in your goals and dreams is to be blessed more than those who do not acknowledge Him. Without God, there can be neither true happiness nor peace.

God is the Author of all good in this life, and you have the right to enjoy it. The Bible says, "But thou shalt remember the Lord thy God: for it is he that giveth thee power to get wealth" (Deuteronomy 8:18). God is the power source to your life's dreams! Since He is the One who causes this world to live and move, why not acknowledge Him in your dreams? He is more willing for you to succeed than your worst enemy is to see you fail! When you see your dreams come to pass and you know that without God's help your dreams would not have come to pass, this will lead you to love Him even more and thus serve and glorify Him. Anything less than this is nothing more than a farce.

The Bible says, "The fool hath said in his heart, There is no God..." (Psalm 14:1). Without God, we would not have the power to get wealth; without Him, our pursuits in life would be impossible to reach. For these reasons, you must acknowledge Him in all your ways. "In all thy ways acknowledge Him and he shall direct thy paths." These words of wisdom are just as relevant today as they were when they were penned.

Use your God-given power of speech to prophet-ically affirm your life's dreams, and give God the praise for the fulfillment of them! *Miracles are just a word away,* and when you have strengthened your faith by the power of prophetic suggestion, you will have power to get out of bed and act now!

Strategy #4
Get Out of Bed and Take Action Now!

Wake up and take action now! Positive thinking, faith, prayer, and prophetic declarations will not amount to anything unless you put your faith into action. Faith is important, and to have a vision and a plan is vital to achieving your life's dreams; but without taking action, your dreams will come to nought.

You must understand that *not* to make a decision *is* to make a decision. Every day we make thousands of decisions affecting our lives for that day. Everything you do is a choice affecting your life for that day and for days to come. You must act intelligently, for the success of your life depends on it.

No matter what the inconveniences are, you know that if you do not fulfill your daily and weekly duties — whether it is paying your bills, putting gas in the car, feeding your children, going to school, and so forth — sooner or later your life will be affected. To lay in bed all day is as much a decision as it is to get up and do what needs to be done.

Today, many are in the bed of their circumstances, desiring better, knowing what needs to be done, but choosing not to get up and fulfill their dreams. They know that they have God-given powers to achieve their heart's desire, but somehow they choose to remain in their circumstantial comfort zone. To them, it is easier to remain in their comfort zone than to risk the pain of exercising their brain, bones and muscles in doing what needs to be done. They remain in bed all day, doing nothing, and finally the day ends and they fall asleep, with nothing accomplished. A day's dream has gone right down the drain.

Jesus said, "I must work the works of him that sent me, while it is day: the night cometh, when no man can work" (John 9:4). The *night* of death must meet us all. We are now in the *daylight* of our lives. Most of us still have time to fulfill our desired dreams. Sadly, some are in the *twilight* of their lives with little time left to work! Many who do have time are still in the bed of their circumstances.

You desire better, but you have not done anything. The day is slipping fast into the twilight of oblivion. You have only one life to live. What a tragedy it is that millions have chosen to remain in their bed, not achieving their potential, their dreams, and their aspirations. They have allowed the day of life to pass them by, and finally they and their dreams will be buried! Scary as it might seem, yet how true it is.

Friend, you cannot allow yourself to remain in bed. The "alarm clock" has been ringing in your ear for some time, telling you that it is time to get up. Sadly, many have chosen to shut off the alarm clock of action and to remain in the bed of unfulfilled dreams. Is this what you want? Do you really believe that success in any field of life can come only by wishful dreaming? If you don't believe this, it is time for you to respond to the alarm clock calling you to take action now!

The alarm clock of action may be telling you to finish school or to receive more education. That alarm clock may be telling you to remove habits and people that will only hinder you in your quest for life achievement. That alarm clock may be telling you to go that extra mile in your ambition and to cross the Red Sea of fulfilled deliverance from the slavemaster of debt, unfulfilled dreams, and so forth. At some time in life, that alarm clock has spoken to us all, and whatever name brand the clock was, it was telling us the same thing: "Wake up and take action, because the fulfillment of whatever you desire depends upon it!"

In getting out of bed there are certain steps we take daily before we get to the fulfillment of our regular duties.

Take Time To Pray

When you get out of bed, the first thing you should do is to thank God for another day of life and to praise His Name, because you know that if He did not watch over you, your life would not have been been spared. Ask Him to bless you with the strength and wisdom to carry out your life duties. This is the first step. Giving God your life each day that He gives you life is the most successful step you can undertake. This gives Him permission to bless and strengthen you in your daily duties so you will know at the end of the day that it was the good Lord who was blessing you.

Get Washed Up

After you have done the first thing, you go to the bathroom to wash yourself and to brush your teeth. This process eliminates bacteria and germs from your body so you can be fresh and clean as you start your new day.

Friend, *many of us need to wash ourselves of negative thinking and the fear of failure.* These two things act as dirt and plaque on our lives, hindering our dreams from coming to pass. You have been given power by God to choose what thoughts come to your mind. The Bible talks about being washed "...the washing of water by the word" (Ephesians 5:26). Wash your mind from negativity by reading the cleansing promises of the Bible.

Negative thinking comes as a result of sin and guilt. If this is your case, read the promise in First John 1:9, which says, "If we confess our sins, he is faithful and just to forgive us our sins, and to cleanse us from all unrighteousness." After reading this promise, ask God to fulfill His promise to you, and then proclaim the truth: "I am cleansed!" The knowledge of being forgiven of your sins is a wonderful feeling. It's like a burden being lifted off.

Negative thinking can also come as a result of a lack of self-worth. *Many feel they cannot achieve anything; therefore, they do not attempt to better themselves.* Friend, the fact that you are fearfully and wonderfully made, and that God put time and thought into creating you is proof that you *are* somebody!

More than that, the fact that God sent His only begotten Son to die for you on Calvary's cross is more than enough evidence that you are somebody special!

God is disappointed when people place a low estimate upon themselves. Away with such thoughts! Think yourself as somebody, not because of anything that you can do, but because of who God is and what He can and will do through you.

Repeat this verse until it sinks deep into your sub-conscious mind: "I can do all things through Christ which strengtheneth me" (Philippians 4:13). As you repeat this scripture, put your name in the "I" part of the verse and repeat it until it becomes a part of you. In this way, you will give God permission to remove negative thinking from your mind and to allow Him to give you His power to think correctly.

If you struggle with fear, you can claim the promise in Second Timothy 1:7: "God hath not given us the spirit of fear; but of power, and of love, and of a sound mind."

There are seven basic fears that hinder people from achieving their life's dreams. They are: (1) *the fear of failure, (2) poverty, (3) criticism, (4) ill health, (5) loss of love or someone, (6) old age, and (7) death.*

Without going into an explanation of these fears, a person can identify at least one of them and see how it might have been a stumbling block in the pursuit of a goal or a dream they had. However, the scripture given in Timothy is a powerful tool you can memorize and use to fill your mind with God's thoughts and His Word, giving you His power to overcome your fears.

God is greater than your fears! Therefore, do not allow your fears to ride you anymore. God will give you strength and power. When you wash yourself from fear and negative thinking, you are mentally and spiritually free to begin your new day!

Make Your Bed

After you have freshened up, you begin the task of making your bed. This is to resolve the finality of your night of rest, affirming to yourself that you are not going back to bed that day. Friend, once you have chosen to wake up and act on your dreams, you must finalize your past by making your bed!

You cannot change the past, but you certainly can change your future. You may be in circumstances where you know you must take action. You might have been laid off from your job, and you are looking for another job or career. You might have suffered a slight setback that could hinder you for months to come. Perhaps you just want a change in life, and you know it's time to take action.

Whatever happened in the past, or whatever you desire to see happen in the future, you must finalize your past and present circumstances and make your bed. You may have to finalize these things by having a good cry. It's all right to cry! God gave us the ability to cry.

You may feel that you have been unjustly laid off from your job; you might have been burned by a failed marriage or a friendship; or you might have made financial mistakes that are haunting you today. Whatever it is, if it is causing you pain, it is no sin to go to your "closet" and have a good cry. Crying is a way to get all the pain out. Thank God for crying!

You need to finalize the past and the present by getting your past affairs in order with people, creditors, and so forth. I do not know what your circumstances may be, but if this fits you, make your bed without delay. Only by making your bed can you finalize your past night of circumstances and go on to higher heights.

Jesus told the man He healed at the pool of Bethesda, "Rise, take up thy bed, and walk" (John 5:8). The man had been unable to walk for 38 years, but when Jesus spoke life-giving power into his being, the man was able to walk. Jesus told the man to take up his bed as a testimony of where he came from so he by the grace of God would never go back to his former circumstances.

Friend, you must take up your bed and walk. Finalize your past and present, and remember from whence God has brought you as you soar to higher heights. Fly above your circumstances. Take action now. *Do not allow anything or anyone to steal your dreams from your heart!* You are a dreamer; you are an achiever. Allow God to speak His life-giving power into your dreams. Take up your bed and not only walk — but fly!

Iron Your Clothes

Usually, when you set out your clothes for a new day, it is necessary to iron out the wrinkles so your clothes are ready to wear. You get out the ironing board and the iron and you start the task of ironing out those wrinkles until they are completely gone.

Friend, before you can start a new day of empowerment in your life, you must iron out of your thinking all thoughts of limitation that would surely wrinkle the beautiful garment of a dream! Iron out the word "impossible" from your vocabulary, because with God on your side, "...all things are possible" (Mark 9:23). Iron out the word "impossible" by starching out the first two letters of that word. After you have done this, you are left with the word "possible." Now you can put on a new life and go on with your day!

Empower Yourself With a Hearty Breakfast

The word "breakfast" simply means to break the fast. We fast from food when we sleep. When we get up in the morning, we break the fast with our morning meal. Doctors have discovered that breakfast is the most important meal of the day. Do not underestimate the power of a good breakfast!

Many have been starving their minds from a good mental breakfast and have no power to achieve big things. They allow the "junk food" of lies and limitations about their own potential from the words of others and themselves to cause them to become malnourished and powerless to achieve their dreams.

Friend, empower yourself with a good mental breakfast! The Bible is the best empowerment book one can ever read. In fact, most books on motivation derive their principles from the Bible. Feed your mind upon the Bible's empowering topics. They will give you strength of mind to carry your life's burdens and to fulfill your dreams. One of my favorite scriptures on life empowerment is the promise in Philippians 4:13: "I can do all things through Christ which strengtheneth me." This is true life empowerment!

When you feed your mind on the living Word, God breaks your fast of empty, limiting, self-defeating thoughts with thoughts that fill the soul with power! Therefore, it would be well for you to read the Bible on a daily basis. In this way, you are constantly feeding yourself with the empowering thoughts of God.

Throughout his book *The Power of Positive Thinking*, Norman Vincent Peale leads his readers to the Bible as the source of receiving power with the thoughts of God as expressed in the Bible. This book has sold millions of copies worldwide, helping people live better lives.

Get Into Your Car and Go!

After finishing your morning routine, you are ready to leave the house, already knowing your destination. You then go to your car, start it, and drive to your destination with faith.

Friend, where are you planning to go on your new day of achieving your dreams? You have chosen to wake up and fulfill your heart's desire. You have gone through the preliminaries; now you must get into the car of action and zoom toward your goal. It may take some time to get to where you want to go, but as long as you apply the gas of faith, the four wheels of faith, prayer, prophetic suggestion, and hard work, you will have no problem getting to your destination. Remember one thing: Don't press the brakes!

Do not use the brakes of fear, procrastination, or doubt to stop you on your way. The road is clear; there are no red lights telling you that you must stop pursuing your dream. There are no speed laws governing how fast you can go. You can go as fast as you desire!

Just remember to fill your gas tank regularly with positive thoughts and thoughts of empowerment so you will not stop short of your goal. *If God is pushing you forward, do not apply the brakes!* The choice is yours: Will you now arise and take action? Don't forget, when you have taken action and have driven to the place of your dreams, you must guard your health.

Strategy #5
Guard Your Health

There is a saying that goes, "People often spend the first half of their lives acquiring wealth, and they spend the last half of their lives spending their wealth to regain their health."

Friend, this need not be. Good health is a blessing. Without it, our mental faculties will be adversely affected, and this will affect our thinking in the pursuit of our life's goals.

The Bible says, "Beloved, I wish above all things that thou mayest prosper and be in health, even as thy soul prospereth" (3 John 2). Good health is a blessing from God. A health expert wrote, "Health is a blessing of which few appreciate the value; yet upon it the efficiency of our mental and physical powers largely depends. Anything that lessens physical strength enfeebles the mind." Whatever affects your physical health will surely affect your mind. The mind is what you use to dream and aspire with. With bad health, negative thoughts and emotions can come, which, in turn, will affect your aspirations.

What Is Disease and What Is Health?

Disease is simply defined by the two words that make up the word "disease." Thus, dis-ease is nothing more than the lack of ease. And the lack of ease is a stressful and disappointing experience.

E. G. White wrote, "Disease is the penalty of nature's violated law...The human family have brought upon themselves diseases of various forms by their own wrong habits. Wrong habits in eating and drinking lead to errors in thought and action."

Natural laws that are violated will surely lead to disease and sickness. To reverse these effects, one must observe the laws of nature that aid the body in maintaining as well as restoring health. *The body has the ability to heal itself.* This is often the case when the body is cut or bruised. Nature immediately goes to work to restore the skin back to its original condition. The same is true with broken bones.

Restoration of health is best done by preventive measures. What it takes to prevent sickness should be used in the restoration of health. The best way to deal with sickness and disease is to restore health. When natural laws are broken, this affects your health. For example, by wrong habits of living, the immune system, which is the disease-fighting system in the body, is weakened. Over time, the weakened immune system is not strong enough to battle organisms in the body, and the result is sickness and disease.

The body is as healthy as the quality of its blood and the strength of its immune system. Good health is obtained and maintained by observing the 10 Commandments of Health. Health is nothing more than the result of obedience to natural law. Remember the law of compensation: You reap what you sow! This law works powerfully; especially when it comes to your health. If you sow bad living habits, you will surely reap bad health; but if you sow proper living habits, you will reap a healthy body.

You Have Only One Life To Live

Many fail to learn much about the beautiful machinery that was given to them by God — the human body. Many take better care of their vehicles than they do their own bodies! They religiously follow the owner's manual for their car, doing all the necessary maintenance — but they recklessly neglect the care their bodies need. It would be far better to neglect necessary maintenance of your vehicle than to neglect what your body needs to maintain good health. A vehicle can be replaced, but you have only one life to live, and you should make the best of it! To waste opportunities for self-improvement in this life can lead to irreparable loss.

To understand the needs of the body and to care for it is essential to achieve your dreams. It would be useless for you to obtain wealth and riches if you have poor health. You would not be able to enjoy the wealth you have. It would be far better for you to have wealth with good health!

There is a wise saying that goes, "An ounce of prevention is better than a pound of cure." It is easier to *maintain* health than to *regain* it. Billions of dollars are spent every year to cure disease. Some patients get better, but many suffer, and some die in the pursuit to regain their health.

So prevention is the best cure. It is better to spend $20 to get a regular oil change than to spend thousands to repair or replace a broken engine! Likewise, maintaining and regaining health is achieved by observing the simple laws of nature that God has established. By doing this, you will have the health you desire and need to achieve your life's dreams.

The quality of health you will have is dependent upon the quality of blood the body has. The 10 Commandments of health is the Great Physician's antidote that will improve the quality of your blood, thereby improving your body's defenses in the maintenance of good health.

The 10 Commandments of Health

The First Commandment: Trust in
Divine Power and Think Positively

The Bible says, "Trust in the Lord with all thine heart..." (Proverbs 3:5). God is omnipotent, which means He has all power. To trust in Him means to give ourselves to Him and allow His will to be done in our lives.

In the prevention of sickness and disease, the use of positive thinking will enhance your health. Negative emotions, such as hate, anger, depression, and so forth, have the tendency to lower the body's defense against disease. To prevent this, positive thinking must take place.

The body produces a hormone called endorphins. This hormone is called "the happy hormone." When the body is happy, it produces this hormone, which affects a person's health for the better. Proverbs 18:22 says, "A merry heart doeth good like a medicine..." The verse continues, "but a broken spirit [mind] drieth the bones."

Science has confirmed the truth of this statement. It was discovered that such negative emotions as hate, anger, and depression tend to affect the bones. They become weak and brittle. This is why your thoughts must be positive: your health depends on it!

God has given you power to think positively. Use that power to prevent sickness. If you struggle to maintain positive thoughts, pray and ask God to fill your mind with positive thoughts. Believe that you are receiving what you ask for. Refuse to think or speak negatively. Repeat such affirmations to yourself as, "By the grace of God, I am well." Speaking positive words such as these will have an effect upon both your body and your mind.

The Second Commandment: Get Plenty of Fresh Air

Without air, we would cease to live. Without fresh air, the blood becomes impure and disease can result. The air we breathe is food for the lungs. The air we breathe sends oxygen to the blood, keeping the system alive and well. Going outdoors and getting a healthy supply of air is essential to the preservation of health.

Many have busy schedules that prevent them from getting the fresh air their body needs, but about 20 minutes spent outdoors daily would do their system good. It is better to get fresh air in the country than in congested cities filled with smog and other impurities. If you are not able to get to a place where the air is clean, do the best you can, and God will do the rest!

The Third Commandment: Get Plenty of Exercise

Many *rust* out rather than *wear* out. Exercise is essential to good health. Our bodies were made to move and be exercised. Without exertion, the body's muscles become flabby. A good walk for about 20 to 30 minutes a day would do one well. Jogging, swimming, and weightlifting are other good modes of exercise. Regular exercise in the outdoors would help many people who are serious about preserving their health.

The Fourth. Commandment: Get Plenty of Sunshine

Studies have shown that plenty of sunshine not only improves the immune system, but it also is a good provider of Vitamin D, which the body needs for strong bones. Ten to 20 minutes in the sun in the early morning or late afternoon have been shown to benefit the body.

The Fifth Commandment: Get Plenty of Rest

There is no virtue in being a night owl! A sound saying goes, "Early to bed and early to rise will make one healthy, wealthy, and wise." When the body gets tired, it needs its proper rest. It would be well for us to get at least six to eight hours a day in proper rest. The best time to go to bed is in the hours before midnight. In fact, studies have shown that the peak hour between 9 and 10 p.m. is the best time for restful, deep sleep.

When the body gets the rest it needs, it gives nature the power to repair it for the next day; but if people observe bad habits for rest, the body is not able to repair itself like it should, and its health will be compromised.

The Sixth Commandment: Drink Plenty of Pure Water

The body is made up of about 60 to 75 percent water. The body loses water every day. Drinking at least 32 to 48 ounces of water a day is needed to prevent dehydration of the body. It is the opinion of the writer that distilled water is the best. Don't forget your water!

The Seventh Commandment: Proper Nutrition

You are what you eat! The body is composed of the foods we eat. Any food that does not properly nourish the body will result in poor health. A diet rich in fruits, grains, nuts, and vegetables is the best diet for man.

God said in Genesis 1:29 "I have given you every herb bearing seed, which is upon the face of all the earth, and every tree, in the which is the fruit of a tree yielding seed; to you it shall be for meat." This diet originally given to man is the best diet for man.

It is well to eat plenty of fresh fruits and vegetables daily in your diet. It is better to eat non-refined grains and breads. Eliminate high-fat foods, junk foods, sodas, high salt intake, stimulating spices, and other things that do not nourish the body. If you are interested in obtaining more information about proper nutrition, I would recommend the book *Counsels on Diet and Foods* by E. G. White.

The Eighth Commandment: Control Your Appetite

Controlling your appetite is more essential to health than your imagine. Controlling the appetite means to avoid everything that is harmful and to use *in moderation* that which is good. Moderation is a good rule of thumb you can apply to food, sex, and work. To overdo something that is good is just as bad as to do something that is harmful.

The Ninth Commandment: Have an Attitude of Praise and Gratitude

Having an attitude of praise and thanksgiving for the blessings God has given you is therapeutic. "A merry heart doeth good like a medicine," the Bible says. The practice of praise and thanksgiving gives health to the body. Practice praising and thanking God for your blessings.

The Tenth Commandment: Benevolence

When we are thankful for the blessings God has given us, we can appreciate the beings that He has created, and we will seek to help those who are in need.

Jesus said, "For ye have the poor with you always..." (Mark 14:7). He has allowed the poor and the unfortunate to be in our midst so He can alleviate their sufferings through us. To those who do this, God promises, "Then shall thy light break forth as the morning, and thine health shall spring forth speedily...And the Lord shall...satisfy thy soul in drought, and make fat thy bones..." (Isaiah 58:8;11). God promises health and healing to the benevolent!

Summary

These Ten Commandments of Health are briefly outlined to give readers something to work with in the maintenance of their health. This information does not take the place of medical advice for those who are under a doctor's care.

These Ten Commandments of Health given by God are simple, inexpensive, and practical for the maintenance of health. They are available to all. These profound principles have been adopted by millions all over the world in their pursuit of health and happiness.

Guard your health with your life; it is something that you don't want to lose! When your health is intact and you have the vibrancy to go after your dreams, you may experience some temporary setbacks in pursuing your dreams, and you may feel the urge to put your dreams on hold, but *do not quit!*

Strategy #6
Do Not Quit

After you have done all you know to do to achieve your life's dreams and goals — after you have committed yourself to God and have trusted in His infinite wisdom to lead you — no matter how long it takes to achieve your dreams — do not quit!

Baseball Hall of Famer Babe Ruth struck out more than 500 times, but that did not stop him from hitting 714 home runs! Michael Jordan missed more than 10,000 shots, but it did not stop him from winning 10 scoring titles, six NBA titles, several Most Valuable Player awards in the regular season, All-Star games, and the playoffs.

Thomas Edison "failed" more than 10,000 times, but that did not stop him from becoming the greatest inventor of all time. Henry Ford spent countless hours designing a V-8 engine and did not become discouraged when his peers told him it could not be done. How wrong they were! These and countless other examples show that whatever dreams you aspire to, if you go the extra mile and do not quit, you are on the way to achieving your life's dreams.

I want to share a poem that inspired me when I first read it. Millions have read this poem over the years, and I think that it would be fitting to include it in this book The name of the poem is "Don't Quit." I pray that you will find inspiration as you read it.

Don't Quit

When things go wrong, as they sometimes will,
When the road you're trudging seems all uphill,
When the funds are low, and the debts are high,
and you want to smile, but you have to sigh.
When care is pressing you down a bit,
Rest if you must, but don't you quit.

Life is queer with its twists and turns
As every one of us sometimes learns,
And many a failure turns about,
When he might have won had he stuck it out;
Don't give up though the pace seems slow,
You may succeed with another blow.

Success is failure turned inside out,
the silver tint of the clouds of doubt,
and you never can tell how close you are,
It may be near when it seems so far;
So stick to the fight when you're hardest hit,
It's when things seem worst,
that you must not quit.

Clinton Howell

The poem "Don't Quit" reminds me of the true story of a poor African farmer. The name of the story is "An Acre of Diamonds." It would be well for all to read this story and apply it to their life as they seek to achieve their heart's desires.

A poor African farmer spent years struggling to raise his crops. The land was not easy to grow crops on. It was rocky and extremely hard to till. Discouraged with his circumstances, the farmer became increasingly fascinated by rumors and tales of "easy wealth" gained by men who had searched for and discovered diamonds in a faraway countryside. Of course, this awakened the desire of the poor farmer to be rich, too.

After awhile, this farmer grew tired of his endless, apparently dead-end labor, and impulsively sold his farm and went off in search of diamonds. For the rest of his life he wandered throughout the vast African continent in search of diamonds. But as he searched and searched, year after year went by — and no diamonds! When it seemed like he was getting close to his dream of finding that "diamond," the great discovery always eluded him.

Finally, after spending many years without discovering any diamonds, the farmer was broke financially, spiritually, and emotionally. He gave up all hope, threw himself into a river, and drowned. Meanwhile, the man who brought his farm found a rather large and unusual stone in a stream that cut through the property. To this man's amazement, it turned out to be a diamond of enormous value. Stunned by his newfound wealth, the farmer discovered that his land was saturated with such stones. The diamond mine that this man purchased was to become one of the world's richest diamond mines!

Do you get the picture? The first farmer unknowingly owned an acre of diamonds! He sold his property for practically nothing, thinking it had no value, in order to look for riches elsewhere. Little did he know that he was standing upon a ton of wealth!

Scary, isn't it? If he had only taken the time to study what diamonds look like in their rough, unpolished state, and he had thoroughly searched the land he owned, he would have found the riches he desired — right under his feet!

Friend, each of us is standing upon our "acre of diamonds!" If you will only acquire the knowledge and wisdom to patiently and intelligently look at your circumstances and discover the gifts and talents you now have, and visualize what can be done with these talents you possess, you will see that they contain the riches you seek — whether they be material, spiritual, or both. Your dream is right under your shoes! Will you now dig deep with faith and persevering effort, to achieve your dreams?

I hope you have been inspired by reading this story. You are standing on acres of diamonds! You must not quit in your quest for that diamond that you are looking for. You may have to dig deep to get it, but in the end, when your desire is fulfilled, you will say that it was worth the work. Friend, many have traveled the path that you are now on and have made it to their promised land of success. Success can be yours if you simply do not quit.

I want to relate a story Dr. Dennis Kimbro tells about the writing of his best-seller, *Think and Grow Rich: A Black Choice.* I hope you will again see what a man can do by the grace of God when he does not quit in pursuing his life's dream. I know that this story will inspire you as it did me.

He Had To Meet Him

After finding out that working for a pharmaceutical company was not his cup of tea, Dr. Kimbro decided to venture out on a quest to write a book concerning "our forgotten heroes — those men and women who had built many of America's most successful black businesses." He set out to compile a list of 35 black entrepreneurs whom he would interview within a one-year period.

This project cost him more than $25,000 in travel expenses alone just to meet these people, but he did not give up his quest. He completed all the writing except for just one interview. It was to be the icing on the cake, but Kimbro was unable to get an interview with his subject, Earl Graves, publisher and founder of *Black Enterprise* magazine. In Kimbro's opinion, not to have included Graves in his book of successful black entrepreneurs would have been like having a bowl of Kellogg's Corn Flakes without the milk! Kimbro, knowing that he had to meet Graves, set out on a quest to secure that final interview.

Kimbro sent his questionnaire concerning the interview to the parent company of *Black Enterprise* magazine in New York City. His request was denied! He phoned the corporate office from his home in Atlanta to explain and to convince them about his need for an interview. Again, he was denied! Month after month of sending letters and requests for the needed interview and month after month of denials!

Friend, what would you have done? Dr. Kimbro stated, "No matter how despondent I got, subconsciously something told me to keep going. 'Stay with it,' I would say to myself, week in and week out. 'Stay with it,' I would tell myself as I reviewed my notes from interviews with everyone on my initial list—except Earl Graves. 'Stay with it,' I thought as I went through my daily routine as a sales representative for a major pharmaceutical firm. 'Stay with it,' as I coaxed back deadlines from would-be publishers. 'Just stay with it.'" Just when it seemed like quitting would have been the thing to do, that "something" — the voice of God — told Kimbro, *"Just stay with it."* And Kimbro stayed with it.

A year and a half went by, and that last interview with Earl Graves was still in limbo. Kimbro thought about completing the book without that "icing on the cake" interview, but he decided to hang in there and give it another try. This time, he gave some serious thought as to how he could get that last interview.

Finally, the breakthrough came! Kimbro remembered a conversation he'd had with a friend of his parents who happened to have met Earl Graves. He obtained the friend's telephone number and contacted him. He told him he had to meet Graves and asked for his help. Kimbro asked the man if he would hand deliver a letter to Graves at a social event they both would be attending. He consented. Earl Graves not only received the letter, but his vice-president called Kimbro to arrange a personal meeting with Graves. Persistence paid off!

After catching a plane to New York City, Kimbro finally reached the corporate offices of *Black Enterprise* magazine. After waiting in the foyer, Kimbro heard the wonderful words, "Mr. Graves will see you now." I imagine this sent not only chills through Kimbro but also gave him a sense of victory and accomplishment. He was going to get the final interview!

Kimbro recalls, "He caught one glimpse of me, complete with briefcase and questionnaire, dropped his notes, and extended his hand in an expression of warmth and hospitality. Then came those words, which I shall never forget: 'Young man, you are to be commended for your persistence. If you are not in sales, you should be!'"

Friend, this is what happens when you don't quit! Kimbro gave some words of wisdom concerning this experience: "Experience has taught me that a man is never quite so near to success as when that which he calls failure has nearly overtaken him. For it is on occasions of this sort that he is forced to think. If he thinks accurately and with persistence, he discovers that so-called failure is usually nothing more than a signal to rearm himself with a new plan or purpose. Most real failures are due to limitations that men set up in there own minds. If they had the courage to go one step further, they might discover the key to the door of all they desire."

Are You Going To Quit?

This is the result of not quitting. *Success is not for quitters.* You have to *go* through to *get* through! What would have happened if Dr. Kimbro had given up in the face of an apparently insurmountable wall? He could have gone on with his project and been successful, but in the back of his mind there would have been a void, because he gave up on his dream: to meet Earl Graves. Thank God, he persevered until his answer came. The same can be true for you, friend, if you will simply hang in there, pray, believe, and finally receive your heart's desire.

I want to conclude with an inspiring statement from Dr. Kimbro which reveals the compensation one will receive if he doesn't quit: "A man or woman who refuses to quit, who keeps going in the face of defeat, who does his best against superior forces, strikes within us a sympathetic chord. The one who does not quit sooner or later will find that nature will give up the struggle against unfulfilled desire and abundantly award the persistent one."

Friend, are you going to quit? I am confident that you will persevere until your dream comes to pass, but remember this one thing above all others: Whatever you achieve in life, this last strategy sets the foundation of all life achievement....

Strategy #7
Put God First

Putting God first, last, and best in all of your life's pursuits is the foundation of true prosperity and life achievement.

Seek ye first the kingdom of God, and his righteousness;and all these things shall be added unto you. Matthew 6:33

Friend, you have the promise that if you put God's agenda first in your life, He will take care of you and your dreams! When you put yourself in God's hands, great things will happen! God is your Creator; without Him you would cease to exist. He created you in His image to reflect His glory. He provides your clothing, food, and shelter. While you are asleep, He protects you from a thousand dangers seen and unseen.

God has given men and women a mind to use to conceive great things. They can achieve their dreams if they only use their God-given powers. You are always on God's mind, and He desires for you to put your life and dreams into His hands so that He may prosper you. If God can do the least of these things, why not put Him first in your life's dreams and pursuits?

From Slave to Head Man in Charge

The Bible tells us a story of a dreamer who, by putting God first, eventually became the head of the greatest nation on earth! The story is told of Joseph, the eleventh son of Jacob. The Bible says that Jacob loved Joseph more than any of his children. Of course, this stirred the envy of his brothers. What stirred them even more was that Joseph was a dreamer. Joseph dreamed of becoming a great man and his family paying homage to him. In his innocence, Joseph revealed this dream to his brothers, and this aroused more anger against him. Be careful to whom you reveal your dreams!

The Bible goes on to say that Joseph was sold into slavery in Egypt. His brothers had plotted to kill him, but instead they sold him into Egyptian slavery. This was a terrible calamity to Joseph, but he decided to put God first when he got to Egypt. The Bible records the results of Joseph's putting God first: "..the Lord was with Joseph, and he was a prosperous man; and he was in the house of his master the Egyptian" (Genesis 39:2).

God prospered Joseph because he put Him first. Not only did Joseph find favor with God, the Bible goes on to say in verses 3-5:

And his master saw that the Lord was with him, and that the Lord made all that he did to prosper in his hand.

 And Joseph found grace in his sight, and he served him: and he made him overseer over his house, and all that he had he put into his hand.

And it came to pass from the time that he had made him overseer in his house, and over all that he had, that the Lord blessed the Egyptian's house for Joseph's sake; and the blessing of the Lord was upon all that he had in the house, and in the field.

Joseph put God first, so God blessed not only Joseph, but his employer's house as well because of

Joseph. This would not have happened if Joseph had not put God first in his life.

Friend, do you have big dreams, but for various reasons you find yourself enslaved by doubt, procrastination, or the hindrance of people with whom you have shared your dreams? Do not despair—the story of Joseph is for you. God is no respecter of persons. He will honor your faith, and He will prosper your dreams if you will put yourself in His hand. He will also lift you up to the pinnacle of greatness!

The blessing Joseph received was not due to any special favor from God. God helps those who help themselves! Joseph put God first in his work, and God blessed the work of Joseph's hands to where his master saw that a higher power was at work in Joseph's life. He also saw that his own house was blessed because of this man whose work was indispensable. Friend, in the pursuit of your life's dreams, give a service that is needed, and do it to the best of your ability. Allow God to bless your efforts and you, like Joseph, will be elevated to that pinnacle of greatness!

The Bible next records a major setback in Joseph's dream for success. Because of a false accusation by Joseph's master's wife, Joseph was put into prison. There are those of us who have pursued dreams and have begun to rise toward our goals, but from nowhere a setback occurred which appeared to bring us lower than when we first began.

Friend, regardless of how many setbacks you experience in the pursuit of your life's dreams, do not give up! There is a saying that states that for every adverse situation a person experiences, within that adversity is a seed of potential that has the power to cause that person to bounce back from the situation and rise even higher. *There is no setback bad enough to keep the persistent dreamer from coming back up.*

Buster Douglas was fighting "Iron" Mike Tyson for the heavyweight championship of the world in 1990. In the ninth round, Tyson with a crushing blow sent Douglas crashing to the ground. Many thought the fight was over, but Douglas got back up and delivered Tyson a TKO in the same round to win the world heavyweight championship! What if Douglas had remained on the canvas, saying, "What's the use?" He never would have known that a few more punches would have gained the victory for him! This shows that if you persevere through your setbacks and defeats, sooner or later the victor's crown will be yours.

The Bible goes on to describe Joseph's being in jail for three years. In those three years, by putting God first, he was on his way up again. The Bible says in Genesis 39:21-23:

> **But the Lord was with Joseph, and shewed him mercy, and gave him favour in the sight of the keeper of the prison.**
>
> **And the keeper of the prison committed to Joseph's hand all the prisoners that were in the prison; and whatsoever they did there, he was the doer of it.**
>
> **The keeper of the prison looked not to any thing that was under his hand; because the Lord was with him, and that which he did, the Lord made it to prosper.**

Calamities, setbacks, and apparent losses could not keep Joseph in that prison for long. After the king of Egypt related a troubling dream, Joseph was called in by one of the former prisoners whose dream he had interpreted two years earlier.

Upon being summoned to Pharaoh, Joseph related the dream the king had had. Because of this, the

Pharaoh released Joseph from prison and made him ruler over all Egypt!. From slave to HMIC (Head Man in Charge), God elevated Joseph because he put God first! The story goes on to say that Joseph's brothers entered Egypt during a drought and paid Joseph homage, not recognizing him. *Joseph's dream came to pass!*

What are your dreams, my friend? Whatever they are, they are achievable! God has given you the gift of life to use in the pursuit of your heart's desire. This powerful story of Joseph has inspired countless believers to put God first, to persevere and to see their dreams come true!

How To Put God First

Because we are created in the image of God, we owe our life and allegiance. We are God's, both by creation and redemption. Putting God first is based upon the supreme law of God's ownership of all His creation. Your life, your money, and your time belong to God, and one day we all will have to give an account to Him of how we lived our lives here on earth. We will be held accountable for what we could have been had we utilized the talents God gave us.

This book was written to lead readers to recognize the God-given powers they have and to utilize them to the utmost to render glory to God for whatever life achievements they desire. When a man realizes this truth — that God is the owner of his life, his time, his money, and his possessions etc. — he has learned the first step in attaining true prosperity!

Commit Yourself to God

Jesus said, "...I am the way, the truth, and the life: no man cometh unto the Father but by me" (John 14:5) Friend, God wants you! He wants your life to be in

His hands. He knows what is best for you, and in putting Him first, He gives some simple directions. The first step to putting God first is to give your heart and life to Jesus. Ask Him to come into your heart and forgive you of your sins. Then ask for His daily guidance in all of the affairs of your life. When you have done this, you are setting the foundation of putting God first.

Commit Yourself To Serving Others

The Bible says, "Love your neighbor as yourself." All men who walk upon the face of the earth are our neighbors. We are to treat them as we would want to be treated. In life achievements, you are to offer a service that people need and to become the best at it. In this way, you are serving yourself to be a blessing to humanity. Mother Theresa, known for giving of herself to others, was loved the world over. If she had shut up her love for the unfortunates, the world would have been robbed of the service she could have rendered.

If you do not strive to achieve your life's dreams and become a blessing to humanity, the world will be robbed of what you could have contributed to society. Do not hold yourself back from others. Give of yourself, and you will be blessed. The Bible says, "Give and it shall be given to you." You receive by giving. *The law of selfishness is the law of destruction.* Unselfish love toward others because of what God has done for you will bring overflowing blessings to your life.

Study the Bible Daily

The Bible is God's thoughts revealed to you. It is the tree of life for a dying world. By the daily study and application of its principles, you ally yourself with life-giving power that will sustain your life mentally, physically and spiritually.

Give God 10 Percent of Your Income

Businesses such as Marriott and Wal-Mart have become successful because of obeying the principle of tithing. The tithe, or the tenth, was ordained by God to sustain the work of the Gospel in the earth. Not only was it to be a blessing to the work of spreading the good news, but it also serves as a blessing to the giver.

God said in Malachi 3:10, "Bring ye all the tithes into the storehouse, that there may be meat in mine house, and prove me now herewith, saith the Lord of host, if I will not open you the windows of heaven, and pour you out a blessing, that there shall not be room enough to receive it." The Lord God promised His people overflowing blessings for obedience to Him upon this point.

Millions of people the world over have received physical, spiritual, and material blessings because of obeying this principle. God gave the principle of tithing to the world as a reminder that He is the owner of all that man has and that by returning a tenth to Him, they are to acknowledge the Creator as the source of all their blessings. From personal experience, I know that 90 percent is *more* than 100 percent! God has blessed me a thousand times over in response to my obedience to Him. If you have not yet done this, why don't you try it, and prove that God will bless you and your dreams.

Take a Day Off — God Did!

In pursuit of your life's dreams, it would be well for you to take a day off each week. Many workers are stressed out because they do not take time to rest. God, who did more work in six days than we will ever do in our lifetimes, took a day off.

The Bible says in Genesis 2:1-3:

Thus the heavens and the earth were finished, and all the host of them.

And on the seventh day God ended his work which he had made; and he rested on the seventh day from all his work which he had made.

And God blessed the seventh day, and sanctified it: because that in it he had rested from all his work which God created and made.

Here God established the foundation of taking a day off each week. He made the seventh day, the "sabbath," the day of rest, not only for Himself but for all of mankind.

God does not need to rest, because He never gets tired; however, as the first entrepreneur, He gave man an example of the wisdom of needing rest. God set apart the seventh day of the week, Saturday, as the appointed time for man to rest and worship. This day was ordained by God to be set aside for man to rest, enjoy, and reflect upon the Creator, who is the reason for his existence. The principle of sabbath rest is truly a blessing for mankind!

In our day, many businesses and people are seeing the need to follow the example of the Great Entrepreneur. God promises blessings for all those who follow His eternal example:

If thou turn away thy foot from the sabbath, from doing thy pleasure on my holy day...

Then shalt thou delight thyself in the Lord; and I will cause thee to ride upon the high places of the earth, and feed thee with the heritage of Jacob thy father: for the mouth of Lord hath spoken it.

Isaiah 58:13,14

Tremendous blessings are in store for all who follow the example of the Creator!

Pray, Pray, Pray

What more can be said? When you pray, acknowledge God's ownership and claim the promise, "If ye shall ask any thing in my name, I will do it" (John 14:14). Ask God for His wisdom in formulating and implementing your dreams. He promises that all who come to Him in faith will have their prayers answered. He may not answer your prayers the way *you* desire, but He will answer them in a greater way than you can ask or think for the glory of His Name. The Bible says, "Now unto him that is able to do exceeding abundantly above all that we ask or think." (Ephesians 3:20). God promises that He will fulfill your desires greater than you think — so pray, pray, pray!

Conclusion

Friend, I am confident that you will succeed, because God has promised success to all who follow His eternal principles of life achievement and prosperity.

The ball is in your hand! You're down by one. You have made the first shot of success, which is your dreaming big; now you must make the most important shot of your life: achieving your dreams.

Doubt, fear, and a thousand other distractions are speaking from the rafters, hoping that you will miss, if possible, the only opportunity to achieve your life's dream. You have put all the faith, prayer, and hard work to come to this point, and now is crunch time.

Aim high, my friend, and expect to make that shot! When you make it, I want you to tell me you have received a Most Valuable Player trophy for your life achievement. This is the next chapter to be written. I look forward in hearing from you that you can...

FLY BEYOND THE SKY!!!!

"All things are possible to him that believes."

God Bless!
Isaac "Dr. O" Olatunji Jr., Ph.D

91

Appendix 1
The One Week
Life Empowerment Challenge!

"According To Your Faith, So Be It Unto You."

For the next seven days, I want you to utilize and prove this life empowerment challenge that will empower your mind, body, and spirit so that you can rise above the circumstances in your life and maximize your performance in attaining your aspirations so that you can truly fly beyond the sky! To follow this exercise successfully, you must diligently follow these simple rules:

1. During the next seven days, refuse to hang on to any negative, self-limiting thoughts, feelings or words. When you feel the urge to think or say anything negative, immediately substitute that thought for a positive one. During this time repeat this affirmation, "God is with me; God is helping me; God is guiding me." In addition to this, pray the inspiration prayer at the end of Appendix 2 daily.

2. During this time, read the Bible promise for wisdom in James 1: 5-6 and pray and ask God to give you unlimited wisdom in how to plan and execute the dream, goal or aspiration that you desire. As you pray for wisdom, ask God to reveal to you any mental

blocks in your thinking that may be holding you back. As they are revealed to you, then ask God to remove them completely from your thinking.

3. Daily read Acts 1:8 and then ask God to fill you with His Holy Spirit for the unlimited power that you need to carry out your dream. Spend at least 10 minutes in meditation and silence and believe that you are now receiving the power that God has promised to give to you. In doing this, you will receive a daily endowment of physical, mental, and spiritual power to carry out your aspirations.

4. For the next seven days, focus entirely on the solution and not the problem. As you do this, you will be amazed at the answers you will receive.

5. If you harbor a negative thought for more than five minutes or you miss a day in prayer for wisdom and power, repeat the cycle again for another seven days.

My recommendation to you is to implement this one-week challenge into a life-long challenge by repeating this same process. You can add or modify anything in this challenge as it suits you.

Remember, the goal is for seven consecutive days! Do not skip a beat! In this exercise, you will:

1. Thereby give the Creator the permission to intervene in your life to empower your mind with solutions and strategies appropriate to your life situation to bring you to the place where you need to begin, execute, and finalize your aspirations. Remember, if you seek infinite wisdom, you will get it.

2. Your mind will be strengthened with infinite power in refraining from cherishing negative, self-limiting thoughts. You will then see the mental blocks that have held you back in the past.

3. You will be strengthened to overcome the habits of laziness and procrastination and you will have power to do what needs to be done and done right.

4. God will be able to mold your life according to His plan. You thereby give Him permission to steer you into the promised land of your dreams!

5. Your life will ultimately be changed! You will form new habits, new standards and new expectations that will help you to grow harmonious — body, soul, and spirit!

Appendix 2
Inspirational Quotations

"Failure to act, is an act of failure."
— Isaac "Dr.O" Olatunji Jr.

"It is our first duty to God and our fellow beings to develop all our powers. Every faculty with which the Creator has endowed us should be cultivated to the highest degree of perfection, that we may be able to do the greatest amount of good of which we are capable."
— Ellen G. White

"If you are not courageous enough to take risks you will accomplish nothing in life."
— Muhammad Ali

"You have to expect things of yourself before you can do them...Obstacles don't have to stop you. If you run into a wall, don't turn around and give up. Figure out how to climb it, go through it or work around it."
— Michael Jordan

"I don't know the key to success, but the key to failure is trying to please everyone."
— Bill Cosby

"The best way to keep people away from you is not to be good at anything. There's so many people who could be good, could be great, if they tried...Some people are scared to risk it."
— Charles Barkley

"You are as good as it gets!"
— Norman Stiggers

"When you realize that you can be your own best friend or your own worst enemy, then you stop blaming others and start to get out of the way of your own progress."
— Louis Farrakhan

"It's not over until you win!"
— Les Brown

"Not to know is bad; not to wish to know is worse."
— Nigerian Proverb

"The rung of a ladder was never meant to rest upon, but only to hold a man's foot long enough to enable him to put the other somewhat higher."
— Thomas Henry Huxley

"He who does nothing to improve himself by the motives and opportunities afforded by this world give the best evidence that he would not improve in any other world."
— Frederick Douglass

"The ship's captain cannot see his destination for fully 99 percent of his journey — but he knows what it is, where it is, and that he will reach it if he keeps doing certain things a certain way."
— Dennis Kimbro and
Napoleon Hill

I can do all things through Christ which strengtheneth me.

Philippians 4:13

I tell you the truth, if you have faith as small as a mustard seed, you can say to this mountain, 'Move from there to there' and it will move. Nothing will be impossible for you.

Matthew 17:20

"Everyone as his own specific vocation in life... Therein he cannot be replaced, nor can his life be repeated. Thus, everyone's task is as unique as is his specific opportunity to implement it."

— Viktor Frankl

"It is in your moments of decision that your destiny is shaped. Therefore choose well."

— Tony Robbins

"Success is a state of mind, if you want success, start seeing yourself as a success."

— Dr. Joyce Brothers

"By taking responsibility for your life and your future and refusing to allow any circumstance, no matter how formidable, to be an excuse for failure, you can create your own unstoppable legacy."

— Cynthia Kersey

Whatsoever thy hand findeth to do, do it will all thy might.

Ecclesiastes 9:10

Wisdom is the principal thing, therefore get wisdom.

Proverbs 4:7

The fear of the Lord is the beginning of wisdom.

Psalm 111:10

"Nothing is more irritating, guilt-producing, and incriminating than an unfinished book; live to your last chapter."
— Dr. Miles Monroe

"Watch the man ahead of you and you'll learn why he is ahead, then emulate him."
— Napoleon Hill

"The cure is in the cause."
— Dr. Thomas Jackson

If thou shalt confess with thy mouth the Lord Jesus and shalt believe in thine heart that God hath raised him from the dead, thou shalt be saved. For with the heart man believeth unto righteousness; and with the mouth confession is made unto salvation.
Romans 10: 9,10

"If you place a low value upon yourself, rest assured that the world will not raise the price."
— Arthur L. Andrews

"Many of us are afraid to follow our passions, to pursue what we want most because it means taking risks and even facing failure. But to pursue your passion with all your heart and soul is success in itself. The greatest failure is to have never really tried."
— Robyn Allen

"Maximize the moment!"
— T.D. Jakes

"There is no substitute for hard work. There will be disappointments, but 'the harder you work, the luckier you will get.' Never be satisfied with less than your very best effort. If you strive for the top and miss, you'll still 'beat the pack.'"

— *Former United States President Gerald Ford*

For the Lord himself shall descend from heaven with a shout, with the voice of the archangel and with the trump of God, and the dead in Christ shall rise first. Then we which are alive and remain shall be caught up together with them in the clouds to meet the Lord in the air, and so shall we ever be with the Lord. Wherefore comfort one another with these words.

1 Thessalonians 4:16-18

Let us hear the conclusion of the whole matter, fear God and keep His commandments, for this is the whole duty of man. For God shall bring every work into judgement with every secret thing, whether it be good or whether it be evil.

Ecclesiastes 12:13,14

Oh that thou wouldest bless me indeed, and enlarge my coast, and that thine hand might be with me, and that thou wouldest keep me from evil, that it may not grieve me!

1 Chronicles 4:10

For more information contact:

Dr. O Publishing
A division of
Dr. O Enterprises
Box 30033
7000 Adventist Blvd. NW
Huntsville, AL 35896
www.DrOEnterprises.org
For orders, bookings or inquiries you can contact
Dr.O at:
Isaac@DrOEnterprises.org
"All things are possible to him that believes"

Order Form For "You Can Fly Beyond The Sky"

Copies	Price
1-9	$11.95 each
10-50	$8.95 each
51-99	$6.95 each
100+	$4.95 each

Quantity	Price	Total
_____	$_____	$_____

Name _____

Address _____

Phone _____

E-mail _____

Make Check or Money Order Payable to:
Dr. O Enterprises